MSU-WEST P|
GARNETT LIB   W9-BPQ-032

Professor William Loader, FAHA, of Murdoch University, Perth, Australia, is a Professorial Research Fellow of the Australian Research Council engaged in research on attitudes towards sexuality in Judaism and Christianity in the Hellenistic Graeco-Roman era. His recent publications include *The Dead Sea Scrolls on Sexuality: Attitudes towards Sexuality in Sectarian and Related Literature at Qumran* (Grand Rapids: Eerdmans, 2009); *Enoch, Levi, and Jubilees on Sexuality: Attitudes towards Sexuality in the Early Enoch Literature, the Aramaic Levi Document, and the Book of Jubilees* (Grand Rapids: Eerdmans, 2007); *The New Testament with Imagination: A Fresh Approach to its Writings and Themes* (Grand Rapids: Eerdmans, 2007); *Sexuality and the Jesus Tradition* (Grand Rapids: Eerdmans, 2005); *Septuagint, Sexuality, and the New Testament* (Grand Rapids: Eerdmans, 2004); and *The Pseudepigrapha on Sexuality: Attitudes towards Sexuality in Apocalypses, Testaments, Legends, Wisdom, and Related Literature* (Grand Rapids: Eerdmans, forthcoming).

MSU-WEST PLAINS
GARNETT LIBRARY

SEXUALITY IN THE NEW TESTAMENT

Understanding the key texts

WILLIAM LOADER

WESTMINSTER
JOHN KNOX PRESS
LOUISVILLE · KENTUCKY

Copyright © 2010 William Loader

First published in Great Britain in 2010 by
Society for Promoting Christian Knowledge
36 Causton Street
London SW1P 4ST

First published in the United States of America in 2010 by
Westminster John Knox Press
100 Witherspoon Street
Louisville, KY 40202

10 11 12 13 14 15 16 17 18 19 — 10 9 8 7 6 5 4 3 2 1

All rights reserved. No part of this book may be reproduced or transmitted in any form or by any means, electronic or mechanical, including photocopying, recording, or by any information storage or retrieval system, without permission in writing from the publisher. For information, address Westminster John Knox Press, 100 Witherspoon Street, Louisville, Kentucky 40202-1396. Or contact us online at www.wjkbooks.com.

Scripture quotations from the New Revised Standard Version of the Bible are copyright © 1989 by the Division of Christian Education of the National Council of the Churches of Christ in the U.S.A. and are used by permission.

Cover design by Mark Abrams
Typeset by Graphicraft Limited, Hong Kong

Library of Congress Cataloging-in-Publication Data

Loader, William R. G., 1944–
    Sexuality in the New Testament : understanding the key texts / William Loader.
        p. cm.
    Includes bibliographical references (p.   ) and indexes.
    ISBN 978–0–664–23161–3 (alk. paper)
    1. Sex—Biblical teaching.   2. Bible. N.T.—Criticism, interpretation, etc.   I. Title.
    BS2655.S49L63 2010
    225.8′3067—dc22

                                                    2010017887

PRINTED IN THE UNITED STATES OF AMERICA

∞ The paper used in this publication meets the minimum requirements of the American National Standard for Information Sciences—Permanence of Paper for Printed Library Materials, ANSI Z39.48–1992

Westminster John Knox Press advocates the responsible use of our natural resources. The text paper of this book is made from 30% post-consumer waste.

Contents

Acknowledgements

This book could not have come into being without the support of significant institutions and people. It distils in part some of the research I have been undertaking as a Professorial Fellow of the Australian Research Council between 2005 and 2010. The detailed research findings have been published progressively over those years and this book's Bibliography lists all the titles thus far. My home institution, Murdoch University, has provided effective and supportive infrastructure, not least the marvels of the modern inter-library loan facility which conquers the tyranny of distance and the isolation of living in one of the world's most remote cities, Perth, Western Australia. I am also grateful to many Uniting Church and Anglican congregations, groups and workshop participants across Australia and New Zealand, who have provided me with the opportunity both to offer input and to listen to questions and concerns.

There have also been special people who have perused the manuscript at various stages: John Dunnill and Ibolya Balla of Murdoch University on the first draft, and Amy-Jill Levine of Vanderbilt University on the penultimate draft, providing a series of comments and questions which helped me shape the final product. Putting so much into a book of small compass has tested my judgement and my patience with myself at omitting so much. At least I can point readers to the more extensive volumes for detailed discussion.

Finally I want to thank the editorial staff of SPCK, Rebecca Mulhearn, Philip Law and Rima Devereaux, and also Jon Berquist of Westminster John Knox, for their patience, efficiency and support. Together we make available a book that will hopefully both promote knowledge and enhance understanding of issues surrounding sexuality, part of human life which inevitably engages us all and where we best find meaning in openness, flexibility and mutual respect.

Abbreviations

4QMMT	4QHalakic Letter
ABRL	Anchor Bible Reference Library
AGJU	Arbeiten zur Geschichte des antiken Judentums und des Urchristentums
ASNU	Acta seminarii neotestamentici upsaliensis
AYBRL	Anchor Yale Bible Reference Library
BETL	Bibliotheca ephemeridum theologicarum lovaniensium
Bib	*Biblica*
BJRL	*Bulletin of the John Rylands University Library of Manchester*
BTB	*Biblical Theology Bulletin*
CBQ	*Catholic Biblical Quarterly*
CD	*Damascus Document*
ETL	*Ephemerides theologicae lovanienses*
HBT	*Horizons in Biblical Theology*
HR	*History of Religions*
HTR	*Harvard Theological Review*
JAAR	*Journal of the American Academy of Religion*
JBL	*Journal of Biblical Literature*
JJS	*Journal of Jewish Studies*
JR	*Journal of Religion*
JSNT	*Journal for the Study of the New Testament*
JSNTSup	Journal for the Study of the New Testament: Supplement
JSOT	*Journal for the Study of the Old Testament*
LNTS	Library of New Testament Studies
LXX	Septuagint (Greek Old Testament)
NICNT	New International Commentary on the New Testament
NIGTC	New International Greek Testament Commentary
NovT	*Novum Testamentum*
NovTSup	Novum Testamentum Supplements
NTS	*New Testament Studies*
RB	*Revue biblique*
SBL	Society of Biblical Literature

SBLDS	Society of Biblical Literature Dissertation Series
SBLMS	Society of Biblical Literature Monograph Series
SBLSemS	Society of Biblical Literature Semeia Series
SBLSymS	Society of Biblical Literature Symposium Series
SBT	Studies in Biblical Theology
SNTSMS	Society for New Testament Studies Monograph Series
SP	Sacra pagina
TJ	*Trinity Journal*
TynBul	*Tyndale Bulletin*
VC	*Vigiliae christianae*
WBC	Word Biblical Commentary
WUNT	Wissenschaftliche Untersuchungen zum Neuen Testament
ZNW	*Zeitschrift für die neutestamentliche Wissenschaft und die Kunde der älteren Kirche*

1

Engaging the far and the near:
where to begin

Issues of sexuality and sexual ethics belong at the heart of what it means to be human and live in human community. Generations as far apart as two millennia share in this reality, although social, religious and cultural factors contribute distinctive ways of asking the questions and hearing the answers. Communities of faith regularly turn back two millennia to explore their questions about sexuality and often find themselves embroiled in heated conflict over interpretation and application. Partly this reflects the nature of the subject matter, personal to us all. Partly it reflects diverse ways of approaching the ancient texts.

This book seeks to listen to the texts in their own setting, both within their writings and within their world. It entails a cross-cultural encounter fraught with possibilities for misunderstanding and with the ambiguities and uncertainties of a strange and distant world. The book offers an empathetic analysis of why interpreters say what they say, including where they may want texts to warrant their pre-formed convictions or where they are simply trying to sort out the historical complexities before them. People having read the book should have a clearer idea of where their feet and others' feet stand and why they stand there.

It is appropriate to begin a book about sexuality with our own expertise. Everyone reading this book is a sexual being. We are the experts on our own sexuality, and how we see our own sexuality will influence the way we see the sexuality of others, including how we read what people wrote about sex two thousand years ago. In the most immediate sense we identify our own sexuality with our genitals, but our sexuality is much more than that. Probably our most important sexual organ is our brain. Our sexual responses are about more than what we do with our genitalia; they encompass also our attitudes, thoughts and fantasies. They can also churn our stomachs, raise our heart rate, quicken our breathing, and much more. In other words, sexuality engages us inside and out. It also engages us more than just as individuals; it engages us in relation to others. Therefore to talk about our sexuality is to talk about how we relate to others and includes our responses both to the actions and attitudes of others and to general social expectations. To talk about sexuality is therefore to talk about society, and to understand what we read about sex in the ancient world we need to understand something of the society in which they said what they said and its gender stereotypes.

Before we begin to imagine that far away society, it is useful to begin with another important factor near at hand. We not only *have* bodies with sexual genitalia, or better, *are* bodies which are inherently sexual; we also have Bibles. That helps define the focus of this book. It is not just about sexual ethics, but about the New Testament (NT). For most readers of this book the Bible sits on our shelves or on the desk in front of us as a single volume. We may be very familiar with it as a whole. Its pages may well show evidence of this, at least their edges, revealing our most frequently thumbed passages. We may even treat it as a single entity, like a great painting hanging on the wall of an art gallery. We may have had the experience of standing before such a work and returning to it regularly, to soak up its impact. It has a life of its own, quite independent of who painted it, or where or when it was produced. It is timeless. In the same way it is possible to approach the Bible as something timeless. It speaks for itself. It has a life of its own. It can be dropped into quite foreign settings or be found in hotel drawers where it lies waiting to address inquisitive readers and draw them into the dimension of God and faith.

The Bible is much more, however, than a great work of art, a timeless treasure. It makes claims about things outside itself, including events of the past and their significance. It makes claims about God and about human beings and proper human behaviour. In doing so it invites us to go beyond inspired impressions which we might take from it as a timeless artefact, to ask what it might have meant in its original setting, to which it also refers. This throws open a number of questions, to which there is a range of answers, some highly probable, if not certain, some very tentative, and sometimes no answers at all. So in our imagination we need to begin by loosening the binding of our single-volume Bible, and to separate the rest from the NT, that is from the early collection of Christian writings dating from the first hundred years of the Christian era. They are, as such, the products of a different time and cultural setting from the Hebrew Scriptures, commonly designated the Old Testament (OT). That is, however, just the beginning. For these 27 writings, with possibly one or two exceptions, also have different authors, writing in different settings over a range of time. Our investigation of what they say about sexual ethics needs to take this into account. To a large degree they are all that has survived from that period, a very small sample from a burgeoning Christianity.

We have, however, much more at our disposal. The NT writings, bound together as one within our Bible in English translation, were all written in Greek. There is always some loss in translation, so being able to read them in the original language is a major advantage. In this book I shall cite only the English translation (using the NRSV), but the investigations which underlie our discussion are based for the most part on reading the original Greek. This includes taking into account the way certain words were used in the language of the time. Beyond mere language we also have access to a number of writings which come from the same period or from earlier times, some of which we know influenced and informed the NT writers, not least those included in the OT. They include also other Jewish literature as well as the works of Greek and Latin authors. Together these enrich our understanding not only of words, but also of the worlds in which people lived at the time, including their sexual attitudes and behaviours.

Our world is very different from their world, not only in the more obvious areas such as technology and scientific knowledge, but also in the arena of sexuality. Most people reading this book will probably belong to typically western societies, where family commonly consists of mum and dad and, perhaps, two children, usually planned, living on their own in a house or unit, secured through insurance or government provision in case of illness, accident or old age, and where one or both parents work outside the home. Our leap of imagination across two millennia lands us in a very different situation. The situation will vary somewhat depending on where we land, but in general families would not be living alone. We would see three generations, and, where it could be afforded, slaves in the household, but much less space. Most work would be done in the household or the land around about. There was no insurance and in most cases sickness or disability spelt poverty. People were mostly beholden to the few rich and their agents and were at their mercy in times of need. Religion played a much larger role in daily life than in most western societies. People were sensitized to what was *taboo*. Values were often shaped by what I call cultic or ritual purity concerns. For those with Jewish background, like most NT authors, these derived from observing biblical provisions about what belonged to holy space, and what in daily life needed ablution and often required the passing of a period of time before purification could be effected, during which people needed to take care not to contaminate others. Menstruation, childbirth, seminal emission, corpse impurity had nothing to do with sin, unless one ignored them. Sexual matters inevitably entailed purity concerns. Sometimes authors use purity language also to express moral values.

There was next to no contraception. That makes a huge difference. There was nothing really comparable to dating. Men arranged their daughters' marriages with other men; so daughters changed hands from father to husband, the custom curiously still surviving today in the old wedding ritual of fathers giving their daughters away. Except for wealthy widows men headed households; women managed domestic affairs. Without a welfare system for the aged, households needed to produce children who could then support their parents and other potential 'burdens' such as widows or divorcees returning home from failed marriages. Male heirs were in most places crucial for ensuring control of property and inheritance. Wives were expected at least to produce sons. An adulterous wife was a huge threat, since she might bring foreign heirs into the family, which could threaten its stability and survival. Securing a good wife was essential. That put a high premium on a woman's virginity, both because it ensured she would not be carrying someone else's child into the marriage, but also because it was a promising indicator that chasteness before marriage would continue as chasteness in marriage. These societal structures ensured that people generally gave much more attention to female sexual behaviour than to male sexual behaviour, except where it, too, could threaten another man's household by adultery, understood as taking what belongs to another man. The unequal focus on women's sexuality still survives in the prominence given to female virginity. Adultery normally meant divorce, as the story of Joseph and Mary

4

illustrates; reconciliation was usually out of the question and even technically illegal; forget marriage counselling!

As we explore the NT texts, we shall uncover many more dimensions of ancient attitudes towards sexuality and their context which will enhance the sense of distance between our world and theirs. Engaging these texts is at one level a cross-cultural encounter where we may apply the principles which belong to any cross-cultural encounter today. These include recognizing that when we meet someone of another culture, there is much more going on than meets the eye. The person we meet may speak a different language, have a different family and societal background, be shaped by different religious and ethical systems of thought, and even use facial and hand movements quite differently or to mean quite different things. Sideways movement of the head in parts of India, for instance, means not no, but yes!

In every encounter with another individual we need to take his or her otherness seriously. We should not assume we can know all about other people, let alone know their thoughts. We will all have had the experience of someone not really listening to us or only hearing what he or she wanted to hear. Encountering NT texts calls for the same kind of respect. Our faith might even reinforce such a stance if it has taught us to respect others. In any case the encounter is about seeking to hear these texts as closely as possible to the way their authors wanted them to be heard. That means using all the tools at our disposal: language, background knowledge, comparison with related material, taking careful note of the context, and much more. We cannot know the minds of ancient authors, so that, at most, we can seek to understand what they have written, all the while acknowledging that such historical reconstruction is always a matter of degrees of probability.

There are no short-cuts, as though, if we take a deep breath of faith, we can somehow sidestep complex realities and 'know for sure'. Wanting to know drives our research and probably accounts for your reading this book. Sometimes wanting to know becomes impatient to the point of jumping too quickly to conclusions or filling in gaps with fantasy instead of coming to terms with the limits of our knowledge. Particularly in dealing with matters of sexuality it is not uncommon for people to become deeply involved emotionally in wanting, indeed, needing texts to say certain things which would reinforce or confirm their own beliefs and attitudes. This can happen from many different angles, both from those wanting to affirm what some might see as conservative positions and those wanting the opposite. The danger, then, is violation of the text in a way comparable to when someone insists that we are saying or should be saying what he or she wants us to say, even when we are not. For others, the engagement has a much looser connection with their own belief systems, so that they are comfortable to agree or disagree, for instance, with what was said. For some, the purpose may even be to depict what is written in the worst possible light, perhaps as a means of becoming more satisfied with their own more enlightened position. Amid all such pressures the discipline needs to be to allow the texts as far as possible to speak for themselves in their own terms. In a spiritual sense it means hallowing the text, treating it as other and holy, in the same way that we respect the otherness and holiness of people, and ultimately of God.

Sexual ethics in the NT is a multifaceted topic, covering a range of issues. The following chapters cluster these issues under five main headings for convenience. There are inevitable overlaps, but the procedure will be to begin under each heading with specific texts. In each case we identify issues of interpretation and the main lines of approach which scholars have taken and why. We begin at 'the deep end' in Chapter 2 with the issue of same-sex relations, which have been the cause of widespread debate and division within the Christian Church in recent years. The aim will not be to propose how people might address the issue today, but to listen as carefully as possible to what is being said as a basis for being properly informed when we need to make decisions. The third chapter draws together a much wider range of texts, beginning with observations about sex, marrying and marriage before moving to some other sources of controversy, the instructions about households in Colossians and Ephesians, and the place of women in family, church and leadership issues of gender. Chapter 4 turns, in particular, to what was seen as disorder, beginning with texts about adultery and expanding from there to other texts about sexual wrongdoing. Divorce and remarriage follow in Chapter 5, focused on very specific sayings and anecdotes. Chapter 6 gathers material pertaining to issues of celibacy, an early cause of contention. In the final chapter we return to a broader perspective, discussing the potential relevance of other foundational issues of the faith of NT writers for both understanding and engaging what they say about sexuality.

2

'With a man as with a woman'

The issue of same-sex relations is hotly debated in the churches and has in recent years produced a jungle of publications. Among these Dan O. Via and Robert A. J. Gagnon joined in 2003 to publish *Homosexuality and the Bible: Two Views*.[1] They are two very different views, Gagnon claiming that 'endorsement of homosexual practice represents the key assault today on one of the church's flanks, human sexuality' and that if successful 'the results would be devastating',[2] and Via arguing 'that homosexual practice among homosexually oriented, committed couples should not be regarded as sin'.[3] This comes, however, after Via's statement that 'Professor Gagnon and I are in substantial agreement that the biblical texts that deal specifically with homosexual practice condemn it unconditionally',[4] which Gagnon does not dispute. They differ not over what the key biblical texts meant – exegesis – but over how they should be applied in the Church today – hermeneutics. We find the same in the analysis of the key NT texts, Romans 1.24, 26–27 and 1 Corinthians 6.9, by the South African scholar Andrie du Toit, who, having concluded that the texts are unconditionally negative, then writes:

> There will also be those who, experiencing the longing to love and be loved, and realising their own moral frailty, may decide on a one-to-one, committed and permanent relationship. They should also be supported in every possible way. Basically we should accept that, while upholding this dialectical tension, if a choice must be made between the biblical position on homosexuality and the love commandment – and such a choice is often inevitable – the latter must receive precedence.[5]

The focus of this chapter is not how we might apply these texts today, but what they meant in their own day. The basic agreement among Via, Gagnon and du Toit might suggest that our walk through the jungle of publications will be rather straightforward. This, however, is far from the case. Via and Gagnon, while agreeing on key texts, differ on others. There are many who would dispute their readings of even those key texts.

It is clear that at least some readers, if not some authors, seek to validate their own hermeneutical stance by arguing that the Bible supports it and so, depending on their special interest, find condemnation of same-sex relations under every possible leaf of the biblical text or find them affirmed even in those texts which apparently prohibit them. In the heat of controversy allegations are made about what distorts this or that author's historical perspective. I will not engage in such allegations. Few of us approach such matters without our own agendas of concern, whether for the health of the Church or for individuals. In exploring the historical material our task is not to pretend we are not involved, but to be clear about our own involvement, and then to set ourselves the discipline of seeking to take the texts seriously in their own terms and context. For those who must have the Bible on their side or must side with the Bible there are special temptations. For those who, still on the basis of biblical principles, are prepared to embrace discontinuity as well as continuity with Scripture, there is not the same pressure, but that is no guarantee that they see any more clearly than others. The commitment we may have to church and people today, which informs our hermeneutic (how we see such texts having application today), ought to convert into a similar commitment to respect our ancient forebears by giving them a fair and humble hearing.

As we walk into this jungle I expect to be doing so in mixed company. While my hermeneutical stance is closest to that of du Toit above, I have learned to respect and to value that people starting from quite diverse hermeneutical perspectives can come together under the discipline of careful historical research and be prepared to recognize approaches of ancient authors which are sometimes compatible and sometimes far from compatible with their own.

'With a man as with a woman'

The title for this chapter derives from the prohibition in Leviticus, translated in NRSV: 'You shall not lie with a male as with a woman; it is an abomination' (18.22); 'If a man lies with a male as with a woman, both of them have committed an abomination; they shall be put to death; their blood is upon them' (20.13). Much has been written about their meaning in ancient Israel, where they probably served a succession of functions, from family rules for survival (procreation), to community demarcation from surrounding cultures, possibly with a view to particular religious practices, to outlawing behaviour in which men were allegedly dishonoured by acting like women, to upholding a sense of order understood not least as divine creation. By contrast, our focus is how they were read in NT times.

Fortunately we have three clear instances of the exposition of Leviticus 18.22. In Pseudo-Phocylides, composed some time between the mid-first centuries BCE and CE, the Jewish author restates and elaborates biblical law in imitation ancient Ionic Greek dialect to pass it off as the work of a sixth-century Greek sage. There we read: 'Go not beyond natural sexual unions for illicit passion; unions between males are not pleasing even to beasts. And let women not mimic the sexual role of men at all' (190–2). Using arguments made by Plato, the author speaks of the 'natural', of illicit passions and animals. He adds women. Philosophers from Plato on often deplored too much passion, Stoics, any passion. Similarly Philo, who wrote towards the end of the same period, gives a lengthy exposition of Leviticus 18.22 (*Special Laws* 3.37–42). He declares male–male sex a much graver sin than sex during menstruation or with an infertile woman. Like Plato (*Laws* 636, 838) he attacks it for subverting what he sees as the purpose of sex, to beget children. First he mentions pederasty (sex with boys), then identifies active and passive partners (those who penetrate and those penetrated), deploring that the latter become female in nature, the shameful 'disease of effemination', and even lose their natural male urge. Stoics at Rome similarly decried what they called the Greek disease, forbidden among Rome's citizens but alive and well in exploit- ation of others, as both its critics and its bawdy entertainments demonstrate. For Philo, partners deserve death (reflecting Leviticus 20.13) for pursing unnatural pleasure and not procreation. He thus applies the prohibition quite broadly to cover not only pederasty but also adult consensual same-sex relations. He does not apply it here to women, though he implies this elsewhere when he rejects Aristophanes' myth of human origins in Plato's *Symposium*, which explains same-sex desire among men and women as the result of Zeus' splitting in half the three forms of humanity, male, female and mixed, so that each now seeks its other half (*Contemplative Life* 63), oddly reminiscent of the divine surgery in Genesis 2.21–22. Josephus (late first century CE), cites the prohibition briefly, linking it to the declaration that the law recognizes only sex between a man and his wife for procreation as legitimate (*Against Apion* 2.199), a view reflected also in the second-century CE work, the *Testaments of the Twelve Patriarchs*, which embodies earlier Jewish material (*Test. Issachar* 2.1–3), but like Philo and Josephus reflects strong Stoic influence. Literature at Qumran reflects the prohibition with little elaboration (4QD^e/4Q270 2 ii.16b–17a; see also 4QCatena^a/4Q177; 4QBéat/ 4Q525 22).[6]

The situation is similar in relation to the incident at Sodom, which depicts violent inhospitality through attempted male rape (Gen. 19.1–29). In our period we find the first clear evidence of interpretations emerging which saw Sodom's sin not only in such violent inhospitality but also more generally in same-sex intercourse (whence our word 'sodomy'). Thus Philo depicts the men of Sodom as overwhelmed by lust for pleasure, engaging in excess like animals, both committing adultery and mounting other men in disregard of what is natural and divinely made. As a result they become impotent, succumbing to the 'female disease', and thwart the divine will for producing children (*On Abraham* 134–7). The *Testaments of the Twelve Patriarchs* argues similarly that the people of Sodom departed from the order of nature established in creation, as did also the Watchers – that is, the angels who sinned by descending to earth and having sex with women (Gen. 6.1–4) (*Test. Naphtali* 3.4–5; similarly 4.1; *Test. Levi* 14.6; *Test. Benjamin* 9.1). Arguably preserving the uncensored text, one manuscript of *2 Enoch*, roughly contemporary with Philo, speaks of 'sin which is against nature, which is child corruption in the anus in the manner of Sodom' (10.2) and the wickedness of those sowing worthless seed, including 'abominable fornications, that is, friend with friend in the anus, and every other kind of wicked uncleanness which it is disgusting to report' (34.1–2). Thus it condemns both pederasty and adult-to-adult homosexual acts as unnatural and non-procreative. The slightly later Jewish writing *Apocalypse of Abraham* depicts the men of Sodom as standing forehead to forehead naked (implying something other than anal sex) (24.8).

When we read NT authors, we need to take into account the extent to which they espoused similar understandings of these texts, but sometimes we are left interpreting silence. This is so with a third text complex, namely the creation stories (esp. Gen. 1.27; 2.20–24), which depict the making of male and female and then their rejoining. Again, our concern is not with their complex origins and possible original intent, from explaining origins to prescribing order, but with how NT authors might have understood them. This includes whether they would have understood male–female sex as definitive and exclusive, a likely conclusion if read in the light of the Leviticus texts, but still an interpretation of silence. By contrast these texts quite clearly serve as a basis for instruction about marriage in 4QInstruction (probably early second century BCE)[7] and the *Damascus Document* (probably late second century BCE),[8] and in Mark 10.2–9. It is unlikely that NT authors read them as definitive in the sense that everyone must marry to be complete, since this is manifestly not the case with those called to celibacy. On the other hand, these stories are foundational for the equation of what is natural with the created order in so many Jewish texts, including those cited above.

Romans 1.24, 26–27 in context

In the NT the two major texts are Romans 1.24, 26–27 and 1 Corinthians 6.9 (also 1 Timothy 1.10). We begin with the first because it raises the issues most clearly. There we read:

> Therefore God gave them up in the lusts of their hearts to impurity, to the degrading of their bodies among themselves   (1.24)

and a little further on:

> For this reason God gave them up to degrading passions. Their women exchanged natural intercourse for unnatural, and in the same way also the men, giving up natural intercourse with women, were consumed with passion for one another. Men committed shameless acts with men and received in their own persons the due penalty for their error.
>   (1.26–27)

These statements belong to the wider context in Paul's letter to the Romans. The first hearers of Romans sitting in their house churches would have come to these verses, having already heard what went before, as would most subsequent listeners. It makes sense therefore to begin with the immediately preceding context.

Broadly speaking Paul is writing to the Romans because he plans to visit them and enlist their support for his future plan of a mission to Spain (15.22–29). He reassures them of his longstanding intention to visit (1.10–13), but also effectively gives an account of what he preaches. Some at Rome probably knew he faced allegations from other Christian Jews of betraying the faith (an internal Christian conflict). So in 1.16–17 he states his confidence in his gospel as good news for both Jews and Gentiles (non-Jews). In 3.21–26 he returns to this declaration and its key words: righteousness (or goodness) of God; its revelation; faith; its universal application. Between these two statements, 1.16–17 and 3.21–25, we find a long supporting argument designed to show that all need this salvation because all have sinned. Paul needed to show that Jews needed this salvation just as much as Gentiles. Both are under sin (3.9). Paul achieves this by describing in 1.18–32 the general sinfulness of humanity, Jews and Gentiles, though in a way that highlights typically Gentile sins (idolatry, same-sex relations) and that would probably have been heard by Jews as typical of their own criticisms of the sinful Gentile world. What follows in 2.1–16 dramatically turns attention back on the accusers who had been so appreciating Paul's statements thus far. The way Paul's rhetoric works at this point suggests that he expects some among his hearers to be caught out, presumably Christian Jews, but just as likely Gentile converts, including proselytes (Gentiles who had converted to Judaism), who had left such a world behind.

Swancutt suggests that Paul may assume his hearers know the allegations of hypocrisy against moralizing Stoic judges in Seneca and Nero's Rome,[9] though one is then left with difficulty in relating them in any specific way to what follows in the rest of chapters 2 and 3, where the focus seems to be not secular community leaders but Jews and Gentiles as people in need of God's intervening righteousness.

Playing games?

If the primary aim is to catch out those who had somehow set themselves above and beyond the Gentiles and depict all, Jew and Gentile, as sinners (3.9), then one might wonder whether what Paul says of Gentiles is to be taken seriously at all or is just a ploy or a kind of role-play. In 1.18–32 Paul would then be role-playing the hypocrite of 2.1 and accordingly such hypocrisy, together with its claims, should be summarily dismissed, including alleged statements about same-sex relations. The problem with that, according to Nolland, is that Paul is not just wanting to expose hypocrisy and, in particular, to show up Jews as sinners (2.17), but to show that all are sinners (3.9).[10] Clearly the sins which Paul lists in 1.29–31 are real sins, and similar to those which he clearly lists as sins elsewhere.

Countryman, who takes Paul's rhetorical ploy seriously, suggests that Paul addresses two different kinds of things in 1.18–32, both the result of idolatry: sin and dirty practices. He takes the Greek word 'filled' in 1.29 as meaning, 'having been filled',[11] and so argues that those filled with the sins listed in 1.29–31 engaged in idolatry (1.28; also 1.18–23, 25). As a consequence they lost their proper connection with God, in that sense, their nature,[12] and got into what, he argues, Jews see as dirty, dishonourable practices (1.24, 26–27).[13] In the role-play which Paul sets up, the hypocrite, then, from a superior Jewish perspective, despises dirty Gentiles and their ways, just as elsewhere he might despise them for being uncircumcised and eating unclean food. Paul does not describe these dirty practices as sin, but only as impure, Jewish terminology for what is dirty.[14] So, far from condemning same-sex relations, Paul, he argues, exposes such criticism as hypocritical. For Paul dismisses such Jewish scruples about food, Sabbath and sex. Christians no longer live under the law but under grace.[15]

One of the strengths in Countryman's position is that it seeks to do justice to the basis of Paul's ethic and his handling of the law. If Paul set aside much of the law, why not also the prohibition against same-sex relations? Its disadvantages for giving an adequate account of the passage are, however, substantial.[16] How do we determine what is rhetorical play from what Paul really means? Nothing indicates that the condemnation of idolatry in 1.18–23 and 1.25 and of sins in 1.29–31 is just play. More importantly, Paul uses the same language there as he does in the statements about same-sex relations in 1.24, 26–27, suggesting he means what he says throughout the whole passage. Thus 'God gave them up to' appears in 1.24, 26, 28, and relates not only to 'desires' (24) and 'passions' (26), but also to 'a debased mind and to things that should not be done (or "what is unseemly")' (28). The latter is then so directly hard up against the list of sins in 1.29–31, that it is difficult to differentiate here between impurities that allegedly do not matter and real sins. The word which Countryman takes to refer to a prior event, 'having been filled' (1.29), is just as appropriately translated to mean: they have been filled and still are filled with sin. Most, therefore, see Paul being just as serious in condemning same-sex relations in 1.24, 26–27, as he is in condemning idolatry and the many sins listed in 1.29–31.

Paul is, nevertheless, engaging in a rhetorical ploy. He sets up those Christian Jews who would join his condemnation of Gentiles with glee, only to confront them in 2.1–16 with their own sin, but not in a way that he takes back anything he has said thus far about Gentiles. Paul, like others of his time, commonly used the language of impurity to address serious moral issues, especially in the sexual arena (e.g. 1 Thess. 4.3–7). There is a certain internal logic to Paul's argument which suggests that he sees a close link between denying God's true nature in idolatry and then going on to deny the true nature of human sexual relations: both are marks of sinfulness and alienation. This is all the more likely if the allusion to those deserving death in 1.32 derives directly from the prohibition of same-sex relations in Leviticus 20.13.

Beginning in all seriousness: 1.18–23

If we see Paul being genuine in his statements in his rhetorical strategy in 1.18–32, we have, then, to examine them in that setting. First we consider the verses in sequence before taking up discussion of key themes.

The good news for Paul is that God's goodness has been revealed in Christ, as he explains in 1.16–17. God's anger is also revealed. In 2.5 we hear of a future day of anger, but here in 1.18 the focus is on something happening in the present. Paul does not depict it here as directed at Adam for sinning and so at all his descendants (cf. 5.11–22), but as directed at people and their wickedness who suppress 'the truth' (1.18). In explaining why God is so angry, Paul claims that they could have known, and known about, God, because from the beginning of creation the invisible God had made his eternal power and divinity visible in creation (1.19–20). This leaves people with no excuse. Instead of glorifying and giving thanks to God, they lost their senses and, thinking they were wise, became stupid (1.20–22) and 'exchanged the glory of the immortal God for images resembling a mortal human being or birds or four-footed animals or reptiles' (1.23). It is widely recognized that we have here a typical attack on idolatry and one closely paralleled in the first-century CE Book of Wisdom (13.1—14.31). It, too, speaks of God's self-revelation in creation as leaving people without excuse, of idolatry as stupidity, and of sin as a result, especially sexual wrongdoing, though it does so in different language and to reassure Jewish readers rather than confront them as here.[17]

A number of aspects of 1.18–23 are important for understanding what follows. First, Paul employs popular philosophical language about nature, which functioned in Plato's arguments. Second, he generalizes. Clearly not all Gentiles, let alone all human beings, have taken the path to idolatry. This is so even though the reference to wanting to be wise may allude to the serpent's temptation of Eve in the garden of Eden. Third, Paul speaks not only of actions (making idols), but also of psychology (darkened and confused minds: 1.22). Lastly, Paul uses the language of 'exchange' to describe what happened. He repeats this idea with an intensified form of the same Greek verb, in 1.25, to recapitulate that they 'exchanged the truth about God for a lie', and in 1.26 where females are said to have exchanged 'natural intercourse for unnatural' (similarly 1.27). This notion of denying what is and putting something in its place which is not true or in accord with reality connects 1.18–23, 25 and 1.24, 26–27. It follows the pattern: deny my reality and dishonour me, and I'll have you deny yours and dishonour yourselves!

Facing the consequences: 1.24–25

At 1.24 we reach the first of the statements about God giving people up (also 1.26, 28). Gagnon suggests that this is like parents standing back and letting their teens face the consequences.[18] Jewett points out that this is forensic language, so that God is handing over the guilty to punishment of some kind.[19] The fact that people commit sin as a result indicates that there is some sense in which God's anger here is understood as letting people face the consequences of their own action rather than that God is engineering both people's desires and what they do with them. That would be to blame God for the sin. Paul does say in 11.7–10 that God hardens people, but here in Romans 1 he clearly assumes that people are responsible both for their feelings and for what they do with them. That shows also in 1.32, which clearly lays blame on people for their actions.

Paul declares that God gave people up 'in the lusts of their hearts to impurity' (1.24). The word 'impurity', as noted above, is not restricted to ritual or cultic purity, but, as 1 Thessalonians 4.7 shows, can embrace moral impurity, including in a sexual sense as here (see also 1 Thess. 2.3; Wisd. 2.16).[20] Paul does not describe this sexual impurity initially, except to make two connections. Thus the words 'in the lusts of their hearts', which could also be rendered 'in the desires of their hearts', continue Paul's interest in the psychological, already noted in relation to 1.21. 'Hearts' here is the equivalent of minds and commonly indicates more than just the seat of emotions. The expression 'desire/lust of the heart' occurs in Numbers 15.39, which the author of the *Damascus Document* employs to introduce a depiction of Israel's history as a litany of sexual wrongdoing.[21] The emphasis here on 'desires' is important, not because Paul sees all desire, and especially sexual desire, as evil, but because he is connecting immoral action with sexual desire that is not properly controlled. Paul is not suggesting that they cannot help themselves, which might alleviate blame, but doing the opposite. One of the best commentaries on desires and their control is to be found in 4 Maccabees, whose theme is control of one's desires, which are depicted as plants in a garden which have their place but should not be allowed to run wild (1.28–30; similarly Pseudo-Phocylides 59, 76; Pseudo-Aristeas 177, 227, 237, 256, 277–8).

The second important connection explaining the sexual impurity is in the concluding words: 'to the degrading of their bodies among themselves'. 'Bodies' is what we might expect, not least because of the reference to 'desires' and to what follows in 1.26–27, which is specifically sexual. 'Degrading' translates *atimazesthai* meaning 'dishonouring'. There is a close relation here between the honour due to God and subsequent dishonour people bring on themselves. Given Paul's familiarity and presumably that of his hearers with philosophical discourse, such shame in a sexual sense could refer to a man being made to take a female role, in particular, in sexual intercourse. That kind of thinking was widespread. It explains the use of male rape to subjugate enemies and more generally accounts for the fear of becoming effeminate, what Philo calls 'the female disease'. The words 'among themselves' would suggest that uncontrolled inordinate sexual desires are bringing shame on all who engage in such acts, including consensually, actively and passively.

Instead of proceeding to spell out this shame in detail, Paul interrupts himself by repeating the gist of 1.18–23: 'because they exchanged the truth about God for a lie and worshiped and served the creature rather than the Creator, who is blessed forever! Amen' (1.25). In fact 1.24 and 25 are one sentence linked by 'who'. Thus Paul continues the sentence into 1.25 by repeating the words of 1.23 ('they exchanged the glory of the immortal God'), using a compound form of the same word, 'exchange'. By employing the language of worship ('the Creator, who is blessed forever! Amen') Paul reinforces the contrast between greatest honour (worship of God!) and its consequence: greatest shame (humiliation of humankind). He is not making a list of sins, the first of which is idolatry and the second, same-sex relations, for the second flows as a consequence of the first.

Instance one: 1.26

Paul's words in 1.26, 'For this reason God gave them up to degrading passions', repeat the sense of 1.24 ('Therefore God gave them up in the lusts of their hearts to impurity'). Instead of speaking of 'lusts', *epithymiai*, he uses *pathē*, 'passions'. The effect is the same. Here he speaks of 'degrading passions' (literally, 'passions of dishonour'); there he spoke of 'lusts' which resulted in their 'degrading' their bodies. Once again the sense is of bringing shame and dishonour.

So far the discussion has been about men, but suddenly in 1.26 we are confronted with a statement about 'women', *thēleiai*, literally, 'females': 'Their women/females exchanged natural intercourse for unnatural' (1.26b). The word, 'exchange', picks up the theme of a terrible reversal. They changed what should not be changed just as people changed the true image of God for idols.

The reference to 'their' women reflects the typically male perspective of the time according to which women belong to men. Paul is no exception, despite his affirmation of their equal worth in Christ (Gal. 3.28) and to some degree his including a discussion of women in this discourse as worthy of attention.

The more difficult issue is to determine what these women were up to. What were they changing? The words, 'natural intercourse for unnatural', appear to employ common philosophical language of the time, which included reference to what is 'according to nature' and what is 'contrary to nature'. Most exegetes identify 'intercourse contrary to nature' in the light of 1.27, where Paul speaks of 'males' abandoning 'natural intercourse of the female' (i.e. with women) for sexual intercourse with men. The parallel suggests that 1.26 is talking about females who abandon natural intercourse with males and engage in sexual intercourse with other females. Contrary to earlier claims, Brooten has shown through her extensive survey of Graeco-Roman and Jewish literature, as well as magical, astrological and medical texts, that the phenomenon of female–female sexual relations was known and almost universally condemned as abhorrent.[22] It would make sense then to see Paul citing the worst and most shameful instance he can think of and which he knows his hearers would similarly condemn. Others have suggested the opposite, namely that he begins with a lesser evil and goes on to the greater one, male–male sexual relations.[23]

This is not the only way to read the statement. The fact that 1.26 does not go beyond the words 'exchanged natural intercourse for unnatural', to explain that this entailed female–female sexual relations, after the pattern of 1.27, has indicated to some that the reference here is not to female–female sexual relations at all, but to 'unnatural sexual intercourse' in general, which could then mean oral or anal sexual intercourse with men, especially as a way of avoiding falling pregnant.[24] Before Brooten's findings this was often linked to the claim that female–female sexual relations hardly received any mention in the world of the time. 'In the same way' which links 1.26 and 1.27 would be about two different ways of abandoning natural intercourse and thereby abandoning procreation, the conception of children. For Plato engagement in sexual intercourse in ways that prevented or had no prospect of producing children was contrary to nature (*Laws* 838) and in this he is followed also by Philo and Josephus, as we have seen.[25] The same emphasis occurs in Pseudo-Phocylides.[26] Sex just for pleasure and not procreation, even with one's own wife, was frowned upon.

Against this interpretation is our lack of explicit references to anal or oral *heterosexual* intercourse as unnatural in literature of the period.[27] In addition, if Paul had given such weight to procreation, we should expect to find indication of it elsewhere, especially where he addresses marriage and sexual relations. In fact, it surprises by its absence. Paul makes no mention of procreation in 1 Corinthians 7 when urging marriage partners not to withhold from engaging in sexual intercourse with one another,[28] and that, despite his own personal preference for celibacy and his expectation of Christ's imminent return, which would render procreation superfluous.[29] The interpretation of 1.26 as reflecting concern with procreation therefore faces problems. If maximum shamefulness is Paul's aim at this point, a reference to female same-sex intercourse is more likely. It is in any case more likely than sex with animals, as some have proposed, because nothing in the context indicates this, though again we are dealing with levels of probability, not certainties, here.

Instance two: 1.27

Paul's sentence continues in 1.27: 'And in the same way also the men, giving up natural intercourse with women, were consumed with passion for one another. Men committed shameless acts with men and received in their own persons the due penalty for their error.' *Homoiōs*, translated here 'in the same way', which can simply mean 'likewise' or 'similarly', ensures that the female and the male activities are identified as similar. Those who see 1.26 as referring to female same-sex acts find that as the basis for comparison. Accordingly both the female actions and the male ones are an abandoning of natural intercourse. Even if the reference in 1.26 is open to debate, the reference in 1.27 is clearly to male–male sexual intercourse. The words 'consumed with passion for one another' translate Greek which literally says: 'they burned in their passion for one another'. The emphasis is on intensity. Again we see Paul's interest in the psychology. *Orexei*, passion, is different from the words translated 'passion' in 1.26 and 'desires' in 1.24, but the effect is the same. It puts emphasis not just on the act, but on what drives it. Again, nothing indicates that Paul is opposed to 'desire' or 'passion' as such. The problem is its strength (burning) and misdirection (for one another).

The words 'men committed shameless acts with men and received in their own persons the due penalty for their error' belong to the same sentence, so should be understood as elaborating what has just been mentioned. Literally they read: 'males in males working (up) shame and receiving in themselves the reward/payback which was inevitable/necessary because of their error/going astray'. Jewett draws attention to the account in Hippocrates of the painful aspect of anal intercourse, suggesting that Paul is making specific reference to this effect.[30] Thus he sees 'shame' here, as often, referring to a man's penis, 'working up' to working up an erection, the 'reward/payback' to the soreness both of the anus and of the penis, and behind the words 'which was inevitable/necessary' he sees a reference to tightness or constrictedness and its effects. Accordingly he translates: 'males who work up their shameful member in [other] males, and receive back for their deception the recompense that is tightness in themselves'.[31] 'Deception', he argues, relates to their sexual conduct as often in Graeco-Roman and Jewish sources.[32] Jewett may well have resolved the problem posed for most commentators by Paul's reference to 'payback' here. Other suggestions range from 'feminization';[33] addiction to same-sex relations;[34] lack of fulfilment; expensive and wasteful consequences in terms of money and time; through to such suggestions as sexually transmitted diseases. The alternative is to see 'shame' here as continuing the theme of dishonouring, present in 1.24 and 1.26.[35] 'Error/going astray' is frequently taken as a reference either to the initial failure to acknowledge God and the run to idolatry,[36] or to the whole process just described in 1.24, 26–27, or to both.

There remain a number of other unresolved issues, which include: Whom did Paul have in mind when speaking of these women and men? What did he mean by 'nature'? What contexts inform Paul's meaning and intention here?

Was Paul talking about heterosexuals and homosexuals?

Boswell had suggested that Paul assumed a distinction between homosexual and heterosexual men and was targeting the latter not the former. He argued that this made best sense of the logic of exchange. These heterosexual men were engaging in homosexual acts.[37] That was an outrage, whereas, he claimed, Paul would have considered it quite inoffensive if homosexual men were engaging in same-sex acts, which would have been seen as natural for them. Most responses to Boswell include an attempt to refute his assumption that Paul would have been aware of such categories, which only entered the modern discussion in the late nineteenth century. This refutation has required some modification as a result of subsequent research, especially that of Brooten, who shows that there is evidence that many people were aware of men and women whose sexual preferences were directed to people of their own sex, including lifelong orientation. She finds evidence in magical practices, and in discourses of medicine, astrology and philosophy.[38] Such discussions are not to be equated, however, with the complex theories of orientation of modern times and are at best rudimentary,[39] but were nevertheless sufficient and sufficiently widely attested to have been within Paul's knowledge. It is difficult to measure whether Paul was aware of such distinctions and then how he might have responded to them, with assent or dissent.

The kind of evidence cited by Brooten is enough to convince Gagnon, for instance, that Paul would, indeed, have been aware of such thinking, and reflected this in his allusion to people as soft or effeminate in 1 Corinthians 6.9,[40] but that he nevertheless condemned all same-sex acts by men and by women. Gagnon argues that when Paul refers to exchange with reference to human beings he is referring not to orientation, as though he meant heterosexuals changing their orientation, as Boswell proposed, but to actions, as in 1.26 where what was exchanged was natural intercourse. If Paul acknowledged that people may have different sexual orientations, in other words, accepted an ancient equivalent of modern theories about different sexual orientations as valid, then he would be arguing that this still makes no difference to the fact that the act is wrong.[41] Thus, he argues, Paul is speaking neither of heterosexuals nor of bisexuals, but of homosexuals. Having such dishonourable passions is no excuse for acting them out. As to how Paul would have understood this (dis)orientation Gagnon ultimately appeals to the fall of Adam. He writes of 'innate passions perverted by the fall and exacerbated by idol worship'.[42] Indeed he argues that 'modern-day theories of sexual orientation are compatible with Paul's concept of sin'.[43]

Alternatively, Paul would have been familiar with notions of innate orientation or sexual preference, but would have discounted not just their relevance to what is sin, as Gagnon suggests, but also their validity. In all likelihood he would have believed ultimately that all people are heterosexual on the basis of the creation stories according to which God made them male and female and/or because this was what he saw as natural. Most who continue even in the light of Brooten's observations to espouse this view see the assumptions of both Boswell and Gagnon, that Paul operated with categories equivalent to homo-sexual and heterosexual as used in contemporary discussion, as anachronistic.[44] According to Smith, most reported same-sex activity appears to have been associated with men who also engaged in sex with women,[45] which, as we saw, Philo supposed of the Sodomites. Via still questions whether Paul did in fact know of such theories, but argues that, if he did, it would be hard to account for why he could then describe it as unnatural.[46] The sin, on this understanding, includes the act, which is seen as unnatural and wrong because it denies what Paul assumes is natural intercourse, and reflects, along with that, a denial by people, therefore, of who they are and were made to be, heterosexual, corresponding thus to their denial of God's nature. This raises the question of what Paul understood as natural, but before we turn to that we need to consider a further alternative concerning what kind of people Paul was talking about.

On the basis of claiming that the predominant concern in both Jewish and Graeco-Roman writers was pederasty, same-sex relations with minors, depicted as exploitive, Robin Scroggs proposed that pederasts are the real target of Paul's denunciation.[47] Support for Scroggs's interpretation has been found in Paul's other main reference to these issues, in 1 Corinthians 6.9, if the terms used there also refer to pederasty. Some have countered the proposal by pointing to the probable reference to same-sex acts between women in 1.26, which suggests an equally broad application in the discussion of same-sex acts between men in 1.27.[48] This would not apply if one took 1.26 as referring to illicit forms of heterosexual intercourse practised by women, but this is less likely.

Scroggs appeals to the major analysis of Dover, who provides evidence of exploitive pederasty as the major form of same-sex relations in Greek antiquity.[49] If this were, in the main, the only form of same-sex relations with which Paul was familiar, then it would make sense to interpret Romans 1 accordingly. Subsequent research, including Dover's revised edition, has shown, however, that not all pederastic relations were experienced as exploitive and that other forms of same-sex relations were known, both in the classical Greek period and in the Hellenistic era, including lifelong same-sex relationships.[50] The extent to which pederasty declined in the latter period and had a place in Rome, itself, is debated, but it does appear to have been a phenomenon among the elite, including Nero, and was attacked as a Greek disease.[51] In Book 3 of the *Sibylline Oracles* a Jewish author already in the second century BCE attacks the Romans for setting up brothels of male prostitutes (3.185–7), and charges a wide range of nations with 'impious intercourse with male children' (3.596–9; see also 3.764) as contrary to universal law (3.758). In the same period *Pseudo-Aristeas* attacks widespread male prostitution in cities (152). Books 4 and 5 of the *Sibylline Oracles*, reaching well into Paul's century, continue the theme (4.33–4), targeting Rome in particular (5.166–8, 387, 430). Pseudo-Phocylides warns parents to take care not to render their boys in dress or hairstyle attractive to predatory men (210–14). We noted above (page 10) that while Philo began his exposition of Leviticus 18.22 by addressing pederasty, he then broadened the scope, and that this is to be seen both in his other treatments and, for instance, in Josephus, Pseudo-Phocylides, *2 Enoch* and the *Apocalypse of Abraham*.

Thus, research since Scroggs has concluded that Paul would have more in mind than just pederasty in Romans 1. In addition, Paul's formulations, especially 'for one another' (1.27), suggest mutuality rather than exploitation and so apparently envisage also adult–adult sexual relations of mutual consent.[52] If Paul stands under the influence of the Leviticus prohibitions, his condemnation is likely to have been comprehensive. That would necessarily also include abusive sex, such as exploitation of male slaves, which, Jewett speculates, Paul may have in mind in relation to Rome.[53]

What is 'natural' and 'unnatural' according to Paul?

In his discussion Gagnon notes that Paul is addressing the situation of Gentiles who without the witness of Scripture should have recognized God in nature, the created world, and should have also seen that it was against nature to engage in same-sex acts.[54] Part of Paul's argument for why God's anger is evident lies in the fact that females exchanged natural intercourse for unnatural and males abandoned natural intercourse with the female and burned in passion for one another. As Gagnon implies, we must distinguish here between the reasons why Paul might reach such a conclusion as a Jew informed by his biblical heritage and why a Gentile without that heritage would reach the same conclusion. Paul is not playing the one set of reasons off against the other, but affirming both. This means that we should assume that he is affirming only those Gentile reasons for seeing something as natural which do not conflict with his own perspective. For instance, to read 'natural' as simply conventional in a sense that Paul would dismiss, would make little sense.

Gagnon speculates that Paul would have in mind as the primary argument from nature the complementarity of human sexual genitalia: the penis fits the vagina, an appeal to visual observation as in 1.19–23.[55] To support this proposal he notes Williams's observation that 'some kind of argument from "design" seems to lurk in the background of Cicero's, Seneca's, and Musonius' claims: the penis is "designed" to penetrate the vagina, the vagina is "designed" to be penetrated by the penis'.[56] As Via notes, however, Paul does not specify his argument in this way, so that at most it remains a possibility,[57] nor does it feature in the Jewish texts cited above. Many heterosexual people, as we would describe them, would have seen sexual desire towards people of the same sex and all actions that might flow from that as unnatural, as they commonly do today.[58] This is usually a pre-rational 'gut'-response to which secondary rationalization is added subsequently. If Paul does not assume a division in humankind between homosexual and heterosexual, then this is a plausible explanation of 'unnatural'.

Paul employs the word *physis*, 'nature', elsewhere to describe the way things are and the right order of things in much the same way as did philosophers of his time, whose language and terms he is employing. This is even true of his statement in 1 Corinthians 11.13–14 that for men to have long hair is unnatural. *We* might define that as cultural convention, as Helminiak proposes also for Romans,[59] but Schoedel argues that *Paul* sees natural as proper, the way nature and creation was meant to be.[60] The incidental evidence of 1 Corinthians 11.2–16 is revealing because it shows that Paul espoused particular understandings of the roles of men and women, notwithstanding his affirmations of their equal worth in Galatians 3.28 and as colleagues in ministry.[61] We have already noted the traditional hierarchy expressed in his formulation 'their women' in 1.24. We might add Paul's use of the Greek word *hypandros* in Romans 7.2, to depict a wife, meaning literally, 'under a man/husband'.[62] Brooten argues that part of what Paul would have shared with his Gentile hearers was a gender differentiation which had implications for sexual behaviour, so that 'natural' and 'unnatural' relate to violations of that order. The use of the Greek word *malakoi* ('soft, effeminate') in 1 Corinthians 6.9 indicates an aspect of the widespread disapproval of men becoming like women. As Brooten notes, Paul also uses the language of shame and dishonour in describing contraventions of what is natural for men and women in 1 Corinthians 11.6–15.[63] The presence of similar language in Romans 1 ('degrading' 24; 'degrading' 26; 'shameless' 27) may well indicate that an element of what makes these forms of sexual intercourse unnatural is that they subvert the norms which govern how men and women should relate.[64] The evidence for disapproval of men taking the passive role in sexual intercourse is ancient and widespread.[65] It is particularly noteworthy in Philo, who in all three discussions of same-sex behaviour cites the danger of the 'disease of feminization'.[66] Given the prevalence of this concern, we might reasonably expect it to be a value Paul shared.

Those who conjecture that feminization plays a role here point to a twofold wrong: allowing oneself to be feminized and feminizing others. It would cohere with Paul's description of such activities as contrary to nature. In relation to 1.26 one would then see as equally disgraceful the converse: women acting as men. That leaves as a remainder women acting as women, but their guilt would be tied up with colluding in their partner committing the disgrace of acting like a man.[67] Thus on this approach Gentiles should have recognized that such acts were contrary to nature in the sense that they perverted the order of creation which saw men as properly in the superior position and women as below them, both literally in the act of sexual intercourse and socially.

We have noted above a further possible basis for Paul's use of unnatural. Many contemporary and earlier discussions reaching back to Plato use the argument from nature to condemn all sexual relations which exclude the possibility of procreation, including, especially, same-sex relations. In this instance, however, the evidence does not suggest that this was Paul's concern. Its only possible foothold in Romans 1 is in 1.26 if women are being targeted for avoiding conception by engaging in anal or oral sex, but most do not read the text that way. We also have no way of knowing whether Paul took into account Plato's argument, espoused also by Jews, that allegedly animals do not engage in same-sex acts.[68]

If the argument about disgrace through crossing gender boundaries picks up the strong emphasis on honour and disgrace in Paul's exposition, the argument that 'natural' and 'unnatural' pertains to passions has an equally strong footing in the text. Paul uses three different words to address them in 1.24, 26, 27 and in addition the common image of burning or being enflamed in 1.27. Following the lead of Boswell, Martin argues that *para physin*, 'unnatural', should be read not as 'against nature' but as 'beyond nature', in the sense of being beyond the usual.[69] Martin does not dispute that Paul condemns such acts, but uses this understanding to develop his view that Paul's concern is not about the direction of people's sexual desires but about their intensity.[70] The reading 'beyond nature' has been widely challenged however in the light of the widespread use of the Greek formulation from Plato on to mean 'contrary to nature'.[71]

While not going as far as Martin, who suggests that Paul sees all sexual desire as evil and marriage as simply a concession to tame it,[72] Fredrickson notes that Paul's statements about desire are important and must be read in the light of similar discussions of his day, which included seeing uncontrolled passions as a major evil. He writes: 'Natural sex was understood in three distinct ways: sex for the sake of procreation (thus only male with female); sex which symbolizes and preserves male social superiority to the female (males penetrate/females are penetrated); and sex in which passion is absent or at least held to a minimum.'[73] He is able to demonstrate that this is the case in both Jewish and Graeco-Roman literature and, in particular, in the context of expressing disapproval of same-sex intercourse. He also points to authors who express the view that same-sex acts are the result of people's passions getting out of control and who, like Paul, also speak of a self-inflicted punishment.[74] In addition he claims that 'Paul is not speaking of the externalization of sexual orientation deep in the individual's personality. Rather he expresses the philosophic view that passion invades from outside and overwhelms the subject.'[75] Paul's repeated allusions to passions in his account appear to indicate that Paul, too, sees same-sex intercourse as the result of such excessive desire.

I find Fredrickson, however, unconvincing in his suggestion that Romans 1 be interpreted solely on the basis of such parallels and not with reference to OT texts,[76] any more than this is appropriate in reading Philo. Jewett suggests that the reference to desires should be read more in the light of biblical tradition than Stoic thought.[77] Gagnon argues that 'the argument from excess passion cannot be considered an argument of the first order regarding why same-sex intercourse was viewed in antiquity as "contrary to nature"'.[78]

In sum, it appears plausible that Paul assumes common ground with Gentiles in his view of what is natural for different genders in sexual relations. This includes (1) what feels natural on the basis of

one's experience or is seen as natural on the basis of external observation; (2) what are natural roles of males as active and superior and
females as passive and inferior; and (3) what is not excessive and ill-
directed. This tells us only part of the story. For though it was enough
to warrant condemnation of the same-sex relations of the Gentiles,
Paul also stood within a religious heritage which could think in a
more expansive way of 'natural'. Thus here as elsewhere Paul's own
values are probably shaped also by his understanding of Scripture.[79]
With a fair degree of probability Paul would have had much in common
with Philo and Josephus and other Jewish writers of his time, who,
in addition to such common values, also equated the way things ought
to be, nature (including what we might sometimes call convention),
with how God made things to be, creation, and rejected excess.[80]

The connection between what Gentiles saw as the natural world
and what Paul saw as the creation, on the one hand, and its Creator,
on the other, is explicit in 1.18–23, and clear in 1.25 with the charge
that they worship the creature rather than the Creator. While 1.18–32
contains no direct citations of Genesis 1—2, the language of Genesis
1.21–26 finds its echo in this opening charge. The reference to
female and male in 1.26–27 then echoes Genesis 1.27.[81] There Paul is
finding reasons to argue what he believes also on the basis of his
reading of Scripture, and that reading appears to include an understanding of male and female and the way Genesis describes how
they relate – and by implication should relate.[82] Gagnon argues that
Genesis provided Paul with common ground with what he assumes
is his argument from observing anatomical complementarity.[83] Such
condemnations of same-sex behaviour as against nature in the sense
of contravening created order are widely attested in Jewish literature,
as we have seen. Schoedel suggests that a shift in 'emphasis from
physical abnormality to psychological disorder aided the tendency in
Jewish and Christian sources of the period to go still further and to
deal with all forms of homosexuality as a species of the same
abnormality'.[84]

Paul's primary argument is that what led to wrong sex was wrong
theology. He employs the common biblical theme of idolatry, even
to the extent of listing categories more applicable to the biblical world
than to Rome, such as worship of birds, animals and reptiles. His
Jewish tradition connected idolatry with descent into sexual wrongdoing, illustrated in Wisdom 13—15. As Martin emphasizes against

Hays, the line of argument proceeds not from the fall – which scarcely features here as it does in 5.12–23 – to sexual immorality, but from idolatry.[85] Gagnon concedes this and criticizes Hays on this account,[86] though Gagnon still argues that the fall lies in the background,[87] including as the explanation for the origin of what he understands as dishonourable homosexual passions.[88] Others see Paul using the creation stories more like the Jewish writers of the time as the basis for denying the validity of both same-sex acts and same-sex passions as unnatural and contrary to God's order.

The other element of Scripture which Paul's discourse appears to presuppose is the prohibition found in Leviticus 18.22 and 20.13, even if they are nowhere cited, though the statement in 1.32 that those who practise such things are worthy of death probably alludes to Leviticus 20.13.[89] The prohibition features in a major way in the discussions in Philo and Josephus and also in Pseudo-Phocylides, as we have seen. Very probably, then, this prohibition also shaped Paul's intent in Romans 1. If Paul assumed the Leviticus prohibition was universal and interpreted the creation stories as depicting what is in right order and natural, then one might expect, as Gagnon argues, that he would condemn all forms of same-sex intercourse, not only between males, based on the prohibitions in Leviticus and his under-standing of the order of creation as natural, but also between females, based on the latter, just as did Pseudo-Phocylides and, by implication, Philo.[90] Nolland observes: 'Paul is likely to have drawn a line from "male and female he created them" to the Leviticus texts and gained from this link his confidence that this bit of the law applied to Gentiles as well.'[91] The Leviticus texts also speak of 'males'. As Brooten puts it, 'Rom 1.26f reflects the Jewish legal thinking concerning same-sex love that was developing in the Roman period.'[92] Paul's understand-ing reflects the influence of Scripture and its laws. Here Via, Gagnon, Brooten, du Toit, and many others who may reach very different hermeneutical conclusions, agree and rightly so. Thus Via speaks of same-sex relations according to Paul as being 'contrary to the order of the world as created by God'[93] and du Toit of three lines converging: (1) 'what the normal, heterosexual majority of his readers, on account of their own sexual orientation, would regard as natural'; (2) 'what the conservatives in the Greco-Roman world, as represented by their moralists, would view as "natural"'; and as decisive (3) 'conformity to the will of God'.[94]

Romans 1 in context

The strength of research on Romans 1 has been the extent to which scholars have identified what Paul might have meant in the light of what we know as his context. Its weakness is probably to be found where this context has been too narrowly defined or where restrictions have been placed on what is likely to have influenced Paul. There appears to be a strong case for influence both from his Jewish biblical heritage and from contemporary Jewish and Graeco-Roman discussions. Perhaps with the exception of concern with procreation, though even that is debated, and concern about pleasure in itself, which appears not to bother Paul,[95] most contemporary concerns can be plausibly shown to play a role. That includes the prohibitions of Leviticus understood as universal, the notion of created order of humankind as male and female and of intercourse as between the sexes, the gross impact of uncontrolled passions which lead to same-sex acts, and the shamefulness and disgrace when a man is feminized and a woman usurps male position. Concern with pederasty and exploitation is not immediately evident, but certainly to be included within what appears as blanket disapproval.

Paul appears intent on evoking revulsion on the basis of what he describes[96] and assumes he will succeed. Nothing suggests that he is developing new ideas here. It is in his interest to appeal to the spirit of condemnation he can assume, in order for his challenge in 2.1 to work. In this sense, while serious and deplorable in his view, same-sex intercourse is incidental to his argument and larger concerns, but well suited to show the connection between what he sees as perversion of the natural in each case. As du Toit notes, Paul does not return to this theme elsewhere, so that we should not see its place in the argument of Romans as indicating that he saw it as the grossest of all sins.[97] Even if one might argue that all of Paul's generalized references to sexual immorality would imply it, he does not single it out, and where he does identify the theme, namely in 1 Corinthians 6.9, it comes somewhat down the list.

1 Corinthians 6.9

In the context of confronting the Corinthians who have been taking each other to court before secular judges, Paul protests that they should deal with their disputes within the Christian community (6.1–8). Somewhat disparagingly he disqualifies unbelieving judges as unjust and then declares in support of his charge: 'Do you not know that wrongdoers will not inherit the kingdom of God? Do not be deceived! Fornicators, idolaters, adulterers, *malakoi*, *arsenokoitai*, thieves, the greedy, drunkards, revilers, robbers – none of these will inherit the kingdom of God' (6.9–10). I cite the NRSV here with the exception of the two words which it translates 'male prostitutes' and 'sodomites'. The meaning of both words is far from clear and certainly not as clear as this translation presupposes.

The Greek word *malakoi* is widely attested and basically means 'soft'. Applied to men it is frequently pejorative, indicating effeminacy, something shameful among men.[98] It could therefore be used in a sexual sense of men who took the female role in sexual intercourse, which was assumed to be passive and weak,[99] but was not a technical term in this sense. The word group appears in sexual contexts with reference to boys in puberty whom men might find attractive as a sexual partner; (usually young) men who were rendered attractive by force, including by castration, imposed dress and cosmetics; adult males who did so of their own accord; or (usually young) men who either voluntarily or otherwise functioned as male prostitutes. Paul uses the word in an obviously disapproving way, setting such persons beside adulterers, idolaters and sexual wrongdoers, on the one side, and thieves, drunkards, revilers, robbers, on the other. It is very difficult to narrow down Paul's meaning here, not least because of the wide range of possibilities and the fact that the word occurs in a list and is not the focus of special attention. On the basis of much later usage Boswell proposed that it referred to masturbators.[100] Citing contemporary literature, Martin argues that it more likely refers to effeminacy in a broad sense, particularly with a view to abuses often associated with it, which might include same-sex relations, but could include much more than that, such as indulgence in luxury and possibly also improper ways of engaging sexually with women.[101] Most narrow their understanding to the sexual on grounds that they see effeminacy in itself as not warranting the severity of Paul's censure here and so see it as referring to the so-called passive partner in male–male sexual intercourse.[102] Some go beyond this to specify one or other of the options mentioned above, but this really amounts to pressing possibilities into something more, since we lack sufficient evidence. At most one could argue that Paul could have used specific terms if he meant a distinctive practice.[103] One factor which people have, however, seen as potentially casting more light on the meaning of *malakoi* is the word which immediately follows it: *arsenokoitai*.

This word is unknown in literature before Paul. Paul assumes it is comprehensible to his hearers.[104] This suggests he has not invented the word on the spot, but that it is nevertheless a relatively recent invention, in which case its etymology is likely to be of significance. Two factors suggest that it has a sexual reference. The word is made up of 'bed' (*koit*) and 'male' (*arseno*), suggesting sexual intercourse involving males. The juxtaposition to *malakoi*, if it has same-sex connotations, would support this conclusion. Boswell argued that it referred to a male bedding anyone else, male or female, and probably referred to male prostitutes.[105] Most see it as referring to males bedding males. In tracing use of the word in subsequent writings Martin notes that in four of its earliest occurrences it appears to be associated with violence and exploitation, rather than just sexual wrongdoing.[106] This suggests that in these contexts, at least, it refers to men who exploit other males for sex, either by violence or in some other way, which might include prostitution, although that need not have been understood as exploitive in all instances. Elliott notes that in Polycarp 5.3 it is associated with craving which should be avoided.[107] Scroggs suggests that the word derives from a development already in Hebrew which he traces in rabbinic literature (*b. Sabb.* 17b; *b. Sukkah* 29a; *b. Sanh.* 82a), where *miškan zakûr* in Leviticus 18.22 and 20.13 gave rise to the term,[108] though his evidence is late. He sees here a reference to a male employing a boy prostitute.[109] Others have suggested a more direct route according to which the word was formed on the basis of the Greek translation of these texts, which uses the same terminology (*koit* and *arsen*),[110] though this cannot be claimed with certainty.[111] Then the term would probably be understood by those who first used it as naming those who contravened these prohibitions, and, where these were understood as universal, referring to all men who engage in sex with other men, whatever their age or status. In other words it would encompass everyone from adult citizens engaging with one another freely, through to pederasty and prostitution, a general condemnation such as we find in Romans 1.[112] If this is its intent, then it is likely that we should read *malakoi* in that light, so that the two words would refer to the passive and active participants in all same-sex relations or some form of them, commercial or/and abusive.[113] Paul could, however, have nuanced them otherwise. They do not appear as a pair elsewhere[114] and may be juxtaposed here simply on stylistic grounds, given Paul's propensity for shaping lists by sound as much as content.[115] Possibly Paul has that whole range of same-sex relations in mind here or possibly particular kinds which would especially illustrate what he means here by 'unjust', although he used that term rather widely as the rest of the list indicates and he might have used more specific terms if he had a narrower sense in mind.[116] It is impossible to know for sure.

The only other NT use of *arsenokoitai* comes in a later work, composed in Paul's name, where we read:

> This means understanding that the law is laid down not for the inno-cent but for the lawless and disobedient, for the godless and sinful, for the unholy and profane, for those who kill their father or mother, for murderers, fornicators, *arsenokoitai*, slave traders, liars, perjurers, and whatever else is contrary to the sound teaching that conforms to the glorious gospel of the blessed God, which he entrusted to me.
>
> (1 Tim. 1.9–11)

This appeal to the law appears to envisage the biblical law[117] and the list follows the order of the Decalogue: 'Honor your father and your mother…You shall not murder. Neither shall you commit adultery. Neither shall you steal. Neither shall you bear false witness' (Deut. 5.16–20). The list may follow a pattern known elsewhere of using each prohibition as an umbrella under which to gather related con-cerns. This was commonly the case with 'adultery'. Here the word 'fornicators' translates *pornois* which originally meant prostitutes but came to mean those engaging in sexual wrongdoing, which would include adultery and much more. If *arsenokoitai* here refers gener-ally to men engaging in same-sex intercourse, then the pairing is similar to what we find in Pseudo-Phocylides, which in elaborating the prohibition reads: 'Neither commit adultery nor rouse passion for males' (3). Scroggs, however, suggests that the connection may be just as much to the prohibition of stealing, expressed here only as 'slave-traders', especially if part of the slave trade included enslaving young men as prostitutes.[118] He suggests that this connection might be reinforced if we read the previous word in its earlier more restricted sense as referring to prostitutes. Even leaving that aside as a possibility, the two words *arsenokoitai* and 'slave traders' would address aspects identified differently in one reading of 1 Corinthians 6.9, but in reverse order, namely those engaged actively and those engaged passively, but focus on the passive partner not as one to be condemned but as a victim of slave traders. It would cohere then with Martin's observation noted above that in some of its early uses *arsenokoitai* implies some kind of violence. Given the appeal to the biblical law in the preceding verses the author would have understood these as particular instances coming within a broad prohibition of same-sex relations among men. But this reconstruction must also be treated with caution. It is equally possible that *arsenokoitai* does not sit under two umbrellas at all, stealing and sexual wrongdoing, but just under the latter, slave traders being condemned on much broader grounds.

Elsewhere in the New Testament

Beyond these three texts we find no further references to same-sex relations in the NT. This has not stopped speculation that it could be implied elsewhere. Jude 6–7 refers to Sodom's sexual sin as going literally 'after strange flesh', which could imply same-sex relations,[119] if it does not refer to angels. In Matthew 10.14–15 // Luke 10.10–12 Sodom's inhospitality is the focus, not sex.[120] In Mark 10.2–9 // Matthew 19.3–9 Jesus uses Genesis 1.27 and 2.24 as norm for marriage and ground for rejecting divorce, not to address same-sex relations, though he may well have understood these as excluding all other sexual relations.[121] Jesus' employment of the image of the eunuch to explain and perhaps defend his own choice not to marry (19.11–12) reflects awareness that some people were eunuchs from birth, thus not sitting easily within the categories of male and female as some defined them and not able to perform what some then and now declare as the norm. But whether some of these might have had sexual preferences for people of their own sex is a possibility about which to speculate but can be no more than that.[122] Speculation that the centurion's servant must be his slave also in a sexual sense, applicable at most only in Matthew 8.5–13 and Luke 7.1–10, but not in John 4.46–54, where the boy is described as the official's son,[123] is most improbable, as are readings of Jesus' relation with the beloved disciple in the Fourth Gospel as homoerotic.[124] The warning about causing little ones to stumble (Mark 9.42) may have alluded to pederasty, despite its later application to believers,[125] and the anecdote about bringing children to Jesus that he might touch them, which evokes the disciples' stern rebuke (Mark 10.13–15), could be heard in certain contexts as a rejection of pederasty, but this is highly speculative.[126]

Generalizing condemnations of sexual wrongdoing such as we find in the list in Mark 7.20–21 and similar lists,[127] where clearly sexual concerns have prominence, often reflecting their order of the Decalogue, would probably have implied prohibition of same-sex relations along with similar prohibitions in Leviticus 18, as in Acts 15.29.[128] This is still an argument from silence, as are appeals to intertextual links between references to dogs in Matthew 7.6 and Revelation 22.15 (cf. 21.8) with alleged references to male prostitution in Deuteronomy 23.17–18.[129] It is possible to read Paul's warning not to wrong or exploit a brother in the matter just mentioned (1 Thess. 4.6), namely Gentile lust, as an allusion to same-sex predatory behaviour, but it more likely refers to wronging through adultery.[130]

Jesus' silence, that is to say, our sources' silence about Jesus' attitude towards same-sex relations, has been read as both approval and disapproval. It probably just means that it never came up or never did so in a way that people felt the need to remember it. The likelihood that he would have shared with fellow Jews of his time general disapproval based on Leviticus is strong, especially if, as the evidence suggests, he observed biblical law, but we have no evidence of the issue being raised, and not all would assume such conformity. The area of sexual mores is one where the early Christian movement appears rather traditional and not to have been in dispute. The exceptions to this indicate a conservative trend, such as on divorce and celibacy; its vision of the world to come as without sexual relations; and John the Baptist's (and presumably Jesus') extremely strict application of the incest laws of Leviticus 18 in relation to Herod Antipas (Mark 6.18). Similarly Paul in 1 Corinthians 7.5 simply assumes that prayer and sexual intercourse do not go well together, on grounds not of morality but apparently of cultic purity, which apparently still plays a role in his thought about sex.[131] In this light it is not surprising that, as most conclude, Paul employs same-sex relations as a proof of human sinfulness and assumes people would then share the presuppositions which led him to that conclusion, however we might assess them today.

3

Model marriage and the household

In this chapter we consider a number of texts which see sexual engagement as something positive. We also consider sexual relations within marriage and marriage within the household and within the structures of society which influenced understandings of roles that men and women were expected to play. Compared with the previous chapter much of the background information which I provide in the initial pages of this chapter is not the subject of great contention. What follows thereafter, however, takes us into texts which have been profoundly contentious, at least in the past, where they have served to support male domination. To understand these texts and their continuing influence, we need to understand their world and to that we turn first.

Sex before marriage

We are sexual beings from the cradle to the grave and the expression of our sexual being is by no means confined to the act of having sex with someone. We are sexual in many different ways. When, however, we look to NT writings for indications of what this might have meant in their day, the evidence is very limited. We must supplement it with evidence from elsewhere.

The NT contains no romantic love stories, such as we know from the Song of Solomon and the Jewish romance of *Joseph and Aseneth*, probably composed around the early first century CE, where Aseneth is hailed as the most beautiful unmarried woman in the world (1.4) and Joseph as a man with whom all the women of Egypt are desperate to sleep (7.3). Jesus' encounter with the Samaritan woman (John 4.4–42) comes closest in form to those biblical encounters which led to the marriages of Rebecca and Isaac, Rachel and Jacob, and Zipporah and Moses, but nothing suggests the encounter is romantic, so that it appears that the author is employing these spiced motifs symbolically of a different kind of life-giving intercourse. Speculation about a romantic relationship or even a marriage between Jesus and Mary Magdalene derives from much later spurious Gospel material and probably a misreading of Gnostic employment of sexual metaphors. We return to this in Chapter 6.

Even references to beauty are few and far between. Acts 7.20 and Hebrews 11.23 reflect Jewish legendary embellishment in depicting the young man, Moses, as 'beautiful', but nothing is made of his potentially sexual attractiveness – which would appeal to male predators and so be negative anyway. The closest to the theme of sexual attractiveness comes in the metaphor of the New Jerusalem, 'prepared as a bride adorned for her husband' (Rev. 21.2) and earlier as 'clothed with fine linen, bright and pure' (19.8). This alludes to wedding attire in which traditionally people dressed the bride as a queen.[1] Sexual attractiveness would have been an element in such adornment. It recalls the late second-century BCE Jewish tale of Judith, who retrieved her festal attire to deck herself out as attractively as possible to seduce the Assyrian general Holofernes (10.3) – to his death! When Ephesians uses wedding imagery it reflects popular values about beauty, including sexual attractiveness, in depicting the Church to be as a bride 'without a spot or wrinkle or anything of the kind' (5.27). On the other hand, corresponding to values of their time, the authors of both 1 Peter and 1 Timothy strongly espouse modesty in dress and appearance for women, discouraging braided hair, jewellery and fine clothes (1 Pet. 3.3; 1 Tim. 2.8–10).

Sex and weddings

The absence of references to beautiful women and attractive men should not lead us to conclude that NT writers must have disapproved of beauty and sexual attractiveness. On the contrary, their appropriateness is assumed, as are weddings. On these, at least, we have more references, including in three parables of Jesus. In what is most probably an elaborated version (cf. Luke 14.15–24), Matthew 22.1–14 employs the imagery of a wedding feast to depict what Jesus came to offer, as does the parable of the girls in Matthew 25.1–13. Such symbolism plays a role in the account of the wedding feast at Cana of Galilee in John 2.1–12, where Jesus made so much wine, as it does in the depiction of the wedding feast of the lamb in Revelation 19.8–9.

The positive use of wedding imagery to depict the good news reflects a positive appreciation of weddings, marriages and marriage feasts as occasions of legitimate joy. The image of Jesus as a bridegroom occurs in Mark 2.19–20 and its parallels (Matt. 9.15; Luke 5.34–35) and also in John 3.29. Getting married was part and parcel of everyday life (cf. also Luke 14.8). That included the joy of sexual union, of which we occasionally find a faint incidental echo, such as in the judgement on Rome, which includes that the voice of bride and bridegroom will no longer be heard in her (Rev. 18.23; cf. Jer. 7.34; 16.9; 25.10) or the possible allusion to the bridegroom's ecstatic shout on consummating the marriage in John 3.29. In such matters, which evoked no religious controversy, we can expect that Christians of NT times shared the best common practices and values with their contemporaries, which were relatively consistent in both Jewish and non-Jewish settings, except for the Jewish limitation of inheritance rights to males.[2] Marriage was very important, reflected in the excuse offered by the man invited to the feast who declared that he had just married, so could not possibly come (Luke 14.20)!

We find only traces of the usual procedures involved in getting married.[3] The process was under the control of men. Even the Greek word for 'marry', *gameō*, has the male as the active party and the female the passive. As the early second-century BCE Jewish story of Tobit illustrates, negotiations about a marriage took place between the fathers of those concerned or their authorized representatives (6.10—7.11). Usually an agreement, sometimes written, sealed the deal,[4] with the daughter passing from the control of her father to the control of her husband (7.11–14), who was usually around 30 years of age, at least ten years her senior.[5] Surviving contracts show particular concern about money and possessions and what happens should the marriage break up.[6] From her family the wife brought into the marriage a dowry of money and chattels (8.21), so there needed to be some regulation in case of a split. The man usually paid a sum of money or gifts in kind to the bride's family, but this was not understood as a purchase price and was often returned to him or them, for instance, in the expenditure of the families on the celebrations. Tobit recounts a simple ceremony where in his own home Sarah's father took her by the hand and gave her to Tobias, saying, 'Take her to be your wife in accordance with the law and decree written in the book of Moses' (7.12), then summoned her mother, instructing her to bring writing material, and wrote out the marriage contract (7.13). It then reports that the men 'began to eat and drink', and, on her husband's instruction, Sarah's mother, Edna, accompanied by tears of emotion, went out with her to prepare the room where the couple would have their first night, where she waited until after the party when Tobias would finally come to the chamber (7.15—8.1). Their marriage had special features beyond the usual, which make the story additionally worth reading, but essentially it reflects the usual pattern: they engaged in sexual intercourse (8.2–8) and a seven-day wedding feast followed (although in their special case it was doubled! 8.19–20).

Patterns probably varied depending on location. The parable of the oil lamps (Matt. 25.1–3) suggests that the bridegroom was on his way home after the party on the wedding night and that the first night was spent there. In Tobias' case, his family home was many days away. Patterns would also vary according to wealth. For the very poor the new couple would have to find a place, if not just a room in the bridegroom's father's house, or perhaps just part of a room, in which to eke out their new life together, whereas the more well-to-do could have a room or unit or dwelling to themselves, which by the time he was around 30 the husband had worked long enough to acquire.[7] Only the dwellings of the better-off, built with lasting material, speak to us from the archaeological record.[8] In the largest of these we find evidence of separation within households of quarters for slaves, but also for the women. In such settings we can make sense of the early second-century BCE Ben Sira's anxious strategy about daughters, whom he so distrusts for their propensity to be sexually wayward that he advises that they remain unseen in public until ready for marriage and then tightly managed to ensure their fathers can obtain for them a worthy husband (Sir. 42.9–14; cf. 4 Macc. 18.7).

Sex and virginity

Not much of the pattern of marriage is reflected in the NT though it can be presupposed. We see there the emphasis on virginity of women before marriage. Thus Paul speaks symbolically in the father's role of wanting to present the Corinthians, as a 'chaste virgin' to Christ, to whom he had promised them in marriage (2 Cor. 11.2).

He does not want them to be seduced like Eve (11.3, based on a reading of the Greek of Gen. 3.13). People placed a premium on virginity. It provided some assurance that the woman would remain chaste in marriage.[9] Men were not under such scrutiny because they could obviously not become pregnant and so endanger the household with the offspring of strangers. Within Jewish tradition, however, there was an increasing emphasis on both women and men remaining chaste before marriage. Thus in *Jubilees* (early second century BCE) Jacob, even at the age of 63, assures his mother, Rebecca, that he has not so much as touched a woman (25.4) and *Joseph and Aseneth* depicts Joseph insisting they not have sex before the wedding (21.1). Paul's lengthy discussion in 1 Corinthians 7 assumes that both men and women are to remain chaste and, where they cannot, should marry.

The best known instance of emphasizing virginity is the familiar story of Joseph and Mary (Matt. 1.18–25). The story is revealing on two counts: Mary was chaste before marriage, but also remained chaste after she and Joseph became engaged. Engagement is not otherwise attested in this period, as Satlow has shown,[10] although this story assumes it. After it had been (re-)established, later rabbinic literature reflects that it was generally regarded as acceptable for the couple to engage in sexual intercourse before the wedding, but that the practice in Galilee appears to have been stricter. Certainly our story assumes it was forbidden, otherwise Joseph could not assume Mary was not pregnant by him.[11]

Polygyny

The NT provides us no instances of match-making or marriage-making, but it does refer to issues of whom to marry. In Jesus' encounter with the Sadducees they with sniggering male humour mock his belief in resurrection by citing the woman who survived seven husbands (Mark 12.18–27). Their example may draw inspiration from the account of Sarah and her seven would-be husbands in Tobit (3.8, 15; 6.13; 7.11)[12] or perhaps the mother and her seven sons in 2 Maccabees 7.1–41. The example assumes the practice of Levirate marriage where when a man dies his brother may take her as wife, providing she is in agreement, a situation potentially leading to polygyny (having more than one wife), where the brother already has a wife (Deut. 25.5–10).

Reference to it in Jewish writings before the rabbinic literature is rare (Josephus, *Antiquities* 4.254–6),[13] but it is nowhere disputed. Jesus' response does not question the practice, but rather addresses the nature of the resurrection state. Polygyny, having more than one wife, was assumed in Israel, though the practice was probably limited to those who could afford it. The *Damascus Document* challenges the practice by citing Genesis 1.27, that God made human beings male and female, and by pointing to the report in Genesis 7.9 that the animals entered the ark two by two, and that royal law forbade kings to multiply wives (Deut. 17.17) (CD 4.20—5.2),[14] but this was probably a minority position.

Ben Sira addresses the problems of rivalry it evoked (26.5–6; 28.15; 37.11), as does the first-century BCE work Pseudo-Philo (50.1; cf. also 42.1–3). Josephus (*Jewish War* 1.277) and Jewish documents from the early second-century CE Babatha archive assume it.[15] In the Graeco-Roman world monogamy was the rule and this appears to be assumed, at least in later NT literature. When Titus 3.5 makes being married to only one wife a qualification to become an elder and 1 Timothy 3.2, 13 and 5.9 applies the same provision to bishops, deacons and enlisted widows, it would clearly be excluded, but there the focus is on having been married only once, not on polygyny. The Herodian family followed the Graeco-Roman practice (which might nevertheless include concubines[16]) and we find no evidence in the NT of believers doing otherwise. Where polygyny was not practised, issues of divorce and remarriage, and to some degree adultery, became more acute, leading to the issues we discuss in Chapter 5 below. Davies and Allison, commenting on the divorce saying in Matthew, conclude that Matthew's community must assume monogyny; otherwise divorce would be unnecessary,[17] but this need not follow. At least, polygynous marriages gave men (but not women!) greater flexibility for what was seen as legitimate sexual expression.

Divorcees, widows and widowers

Usually divorcees and widows, unless they were people of means and received or retrieved a substantial dowry, would go back to their father's household or would remarry. Where these were not options, they faced poverty, from which some could then seek relief through engaging in prostitution. Judith the widow had the means to remain unmarried, despite many suitors, as her tale reports (16.22). This is seen as a virtue. Similarly Luke notes that Anna the prophetess and widow had remained chaste and unmarried to her eighty-fifth year after her marriage of seven years (2.36–38) apparently supported by the temple establishment. In Roman circles there was a growing idealization of people who married only once and as widows remained unmarried.[18] The author of 1 Timothy assesses the situation of young widows (under 60!) differently, advising that it is better that they marry again, distrusting their ability to remain chaste (5.11–14), a failure that gives the Church a bad name and which he designates as turning away to Satan (5.14–15), probably also linked with their susceptibility to false teaching. The accusation against false teachers that they forbid marriage (4.3) probably indicates a strand of Pauline Christianity which promoted celibacy and perhaps an order of celibate widows, the probable context of the young widows' vows (5.12), in which case the author's instruction both contradicts it and undermines the future of such an order.[19] The author's advice also reflected sensitivity to Roman law, which penalized unmarried male citizens aged 25–60 and women aged 20–50 who did not have children or remarry if widowed or divorced.[20] It is typical of the times that we find no discussion of widowers.

Biblical law and ritual purity

Jewish and Gentile Christians sought inspiration in their Bible, the Old Testament. In the following chapters we shall see how mostly its prohibitions are at least retained, if not sharpened. As we saw in the previous chapter, many see Paul reflecting an expanded application of the prohibitions of same-sex intercourse to women. Some aspects of biblical law are concerned primarily with sustaining order and dealing with what were seen as the normal impurities of life. These included recognizing that after seminal emission during intercourse or otherwise a man was deemed unclean until the evening, when he should wash or bathe for ritual cleansing (Lev. 15.16–18; Deut. 23.10–11). This practice leaves no trace in the NT. We have no way of knowing whether it was observed. Non-observance in a Jewish context would surely evoke controversy and conflict, so that the likelihood is that the silence indicates observance. Menstrual blood or related flows of blood rendered a woman unclean (Lev. 15.19–30), so that she should not spread that uncleanness by touch until her flow had stopped and her rites of purification were completed. In the one instance reported, where such a woman touched Jesus (Mark 5.21–43), the story must have assumed that this caused a problem, perhaps earning Jesus' rebuke, as with the leper (1.40–45), but in its present form in Mark this may no longer be significant, since the focus falls on her frustration with failed medical assistance and Jesus' transfer of power. Possibly it once functioned as a celebratory story that such uncleanness no longer mattered. Its embedding in the story of a 12-year-old girl, a significant milestone in sexual maturity, may have reflected sexual concerns, as Via suggests,[21] but that is far from clear. For Mark the number 12 serves to represent Israel as the story forms one half of a two-part panel, the other half celebrating outreach to Gentiles (5.1–20). Issues of uncleanness after childbirth (Lev. 12.1–8) are assumed as still applicable by Luke, who with great emphasis applaudingly reports Mary and Joseph's strict obedience to such provisions, indeed exceeding them in depicting 'their' purification not just Mary's (Luke 2.22–24, 27, 39).

Paul illustrates how closely notions of purity and sexuality were tied together. Even when discussing sexual immorality he frequently uses cultic or ritual purity language. We saw this in Romans 1.24, 26–27. It is also the case in the language of demarcation in 2 Corinthians 6.14—7.1 and in 1 Thessalonians 4.3–7. But sometimes Paul seems motivated primarily by non-moral purity concerns, such as in his advice that marriage partners abstain from sexual intercourse for the sake of periods of prayer (1 Cor. 7.5). The assumption, echoed also in *Testament of Naphtali* 8.8–9, is that sexual activity is inappropriate in the sphere of the holy. In the *Temple Scroll* and the *Damascus Document*, this is the rationale for banning sex in Jerusalem because they deem the city an extension of the holy Temple (11QT[a]/ 11Q19 45.11–12; CD 12.1b–2a), and in *Jubilees* for having no sex take place in the garden of Eden, because it considered the garden a holy sanctuary (4.26; 8.19).[22] In the same chapter Paul may operate from similar purity assumptions in considering that the children of a mixed marriage are sanctified because one partner is a believer, possibly reflecting notions of transmitted purity (7.14), based on the two marriage partners having become one flesh, which Collins suggests contrasts with the negative impact of sex with a prostitute in 6.15–18.[23] As Deming puts it, 'through marriage and sexual relations the holiness of the Christian spreads contagiously'.[24] Alternatively, Gillihan suggests that 'sanctify' here means 'licit' referring to the legal status of the children and their right to belong in the community of faith, reflecting rabbinic usage,[25] though this may still imply purity assumptions about the process.[26]

Fertility, pregnancy and childbirth

In Jewish literature of this general period we find at times a keen interest in the processes of conception, pregnancy and childbirth. 4 Maccabees, for instance, engages such issues to explain the bond between brothers and between mother and child (13.19–22; 15.4–7; 16.6–11). 4 Ezra makes extensive use of analogies drawn from its understanding of the processes (4.40–42; 5.46–52; 8.9–11; 9.38—10.4; 10.14). Wisdom 7.1–2 has Solomon employ it as a leveller: all are born through the same process. Infertility plays a major role in biblical stories, usually as the prelude to divine intervention which reverses it and produces a great hero or saves the lineage (e.g. Sarah, Rebecca, Rachel, Hannah), reflected in Paul's allegory in Galatians 4.21–30, in Luke's story of Elizabeth strongly echoing Hannah's, and in Hebrews' account of Abraham and Sarah being able to reproduce in old age. When Hebrews speaks of Sarah's receiving the capacity to produce seed (*sperma*) (11.11), it reflects the view of conception according to which both men and women produce semen which then merges to form the foetus[27] in contrast to the other common model of the time, which saw the man as planting the seed in the woman – like sowing seed in a field – who then incubated it. The latter appears to inform the account of the virginal conception in the story of Jesus' origins. The pains of giving birth, cited as a consequence of Eve's sin in Genesis 3.16, frequently occur as an analogy in depictions of future suffering in biblical and post-biblical literature (Isa. 21.3; 26.17; Jer. 13.21; *1 Enoch* 62.4). They similarly appear in the NT in association with predictions about the future, emphasizing sudden-ness (1 Thess. 5.3; Mark 13.8) or associated with the hope of new beginnings (e.g. Rom. 8.22). Paul even applies the image to his own ministry and the hope it will bear fruit for people (Gal. 4.19). In Revelation 12 the pregnant woman represents the people of God (Israel), to whom the child Jesus is born, and who then as the people of God (Church) must flee the torrents of the dragon's assault.

Jesus on Genesis and marriage

One of the most important texts underlying attitudes towards sexual behaviour is Jesus' encounter with the Pharisees when they test his views on divorce. The latter will be the subject of Chapter 5. Here, however, we focus on how Mark depicts Jesus addressing the issue of marriage itself. According to Mark Jesus cited two texts from the creation story, Genesis 1.27 and 2.24, framing them with a few words of introduction and a conclusion:

> But from the beginning of creation, 'God made them male and female.' 'For this reason a man shall leave his father and mother and be joined to his wife, and the two shall become one flesh.' So they are no longer two, but one flesh. Therefore what God has joined together, let no one separate. (Mark 10.6–9)

The appeal to 'the beginning of creation' is an appeal to what God originally created and how it therefore should remain (cf. the appeal to creation in Mark 2.27). The allusion to God's making human beings male and female in Genesis 1.27 is not an argument in itself, but rather a presupposition for the argument to follow. The *Damascus Document* cites the verse as part of its argument for monogamy, but that is not in focus here, though on the basis of that parallel Instone-Brewer has argued that the Genesis 'texts formed a well-known proof for monogamy' to which the argument about animals entering the ark two by two (Gen. 7.9) also belonged.[28] The conclusion, 'So they are no longer two, but one flesh,' assumes Genesis 1.27, since it refers clearly to two, male and female. Accordingly, the citation of Genesis 2.24 is seen as explaining how the unity comes about. While some manuscripts lack the words 'and be joined to his wife' and so could have the text referring to either a man or a woman leaving the parental home, their sense is presupposed. The man and the woman become 'one flesh', which means more than becoming kin, an element more strongly present in the Hebrew word translated flesh and which Countryman takes as its sole meaning here.[29] Most see it here as in Genesis as including sexual union. Indeed Paul cites the same text (Gen. 2.24) to argue against sex with a prostitute because, he alleges, one becomes 'one body' with her (1 Cor. 6.16). Beyond the citations from Genesis Jesus is reported here as saying that God joined the two together. The Greek of Genesis 2.24, which can be translated as 'shall be joined', may have prompted this insight or at least have been understood as supporting it, especially if understood as 'joined' by God.[30]

Some important observations flow from this passage. They include the affirmation of marriage between men and women, the affirmation of sexual intercourse as part of that, and the view that this is not just the doing of two individuals but God's doing. One could hardly have a stronger affirmation of marriage, including sexual union in marriage. It also gives to marriage an authority not previously expressed in this way and which later would call for regulation, since this means more than the prevailing practice of the time in which it was simply a matter of people arranging marriages and people marrying each other.

The silences are also significant. The passage says nothing about procreation, such as that coming together in sexual union could only be justified if that is its purpose. Only in Luke's version of Mark 12.25 do we find such values assumed. There Luke has Jesus declare sex and marriage superfluous in the world to come since no one would die (20.34–36), a claim based on the notion that procreation is their sole purpose, a view reflected already in *1 Enoch* 15.6 in scolding the wayward angels who also do not die and therefore have no need of women. Rather the focus of Jesus' appeal to Genesis is oneness, and so, as in Genesis, on intimacy and companionship, including sexual intimacy. *Jubilees* develops the narrative further to have Adam long for the sexual union he observes in pairing in the animal world and God respond by creating the woman and bringing him to her, where his wish is fulfilled and they engage in intercourse together (3.1–7). The passage in Mark does not imply that all should become one in this way. Clearly some, including Jesus, it appears, did not (see Chapter 6 below), and others, like eunuchs, could not. Gagnon is representative of many who see the passage as implying that only male–female sexual unions are valid and all other unions excluded.[31] This is not explicit, though likely to be the case when it is read in association with the Leviticus prohibitions.

Paul on Genesis and marriage

The affirmation of sex in marriage has its roots in the Genesis creation stories. This appears also to be the case in Paul's resistance against giving up marriage and mandating celibacy, as some at Corinth had apparently espoused, in 1 Corinthians 7. We return to the issue of celibacy in Chapter 6, but it is hard to make sense of Paul's resistance to what otherwise is his own personal preference (for celibacy) except on the grounds that he sees marriage as biblically mandated. A few verses earlier he had used Genesis 2.24 against sex with prostitutes. Here he assumes its right application in marriage. As he later shows, Paul does not view marriage as very desirable in difficult times, not because he is concerned with how parents might look after their children, but because he sees the love of each partner for one another as likely to compete with love for God (7.32–35). As Deming has shown, Paul's reasoning reflects a combination of Stoic with Jewish wisdom tradition and a framework of expectations about the future, commonly designated apocalyptic tradition.[32]

With regard to his views on marriage, which concern us in this chapter, Martin argues that Paul disapproves of sexual desire altogether and so 'considered marriage was a mechanism by which desire could be extinguished'[33] and, with Fredrickson, sees the same expressed in 1 Thessalonians 4.4–5.[34] Even then sex within marriage should be without passion. His arguments are based primarily on a reading of Stoic writers of the time, whom he sees as also promoting passionless sex, which then has only one justification: begetting children.[35] This view is strongly challenged by Deming, whose assessment of Stoic and Cynic discussion on marriage leads him to conclude that when 'Martin states that both Stoics and Paul saw the goal of the virtuous person as "to have sex without desire", he is wrong to assert that this excludes love, passion, or romance from marital relations' since both oppose not sexual desire, itself, but its excess.[36] Ellis reaches a similar conclusion based on reviewing not only Stoic texts (Zero, Chrysippus, Musonius, Epictetus) but also Jewish ones on the theme: 'condemnations of sexual desire per se are quite rare. Far more common are, on the one hand, condemnations of sexual immorality (in various forms) and overpowering, excessive, or misdirected desire and, on the other hand, exhortations to self-control'; and he concludes that actual disapproval of sexual desire and sexual intercourse occurs unambiguously only in the Jewish *Sibylline Oracles* Book 1 (late first or early second century CE).[37]

Accordingly at no point does Paul discourage marriage as a place for expression of sexual desire, as though sexual desire were something evil. When Paul writes, 'it is better to marry than to be aflame with passion' (1 Cor. 7.9), some have read this as Paul threatening the passionate with hell,[38] but the alternative is to see him employing a common metaphor of burning passions (as Rom. 1.27; Prov. 6.27–28; Sir. 23.16) and arguing that they are not to be extinguished but appropriately directed into marriage.[39] Later in 1 Corinthians 12.23–24 Paul is perhaps playfully countering a negative attitude towards sexuality when he asserts that our 'shameful' body parts are accorded greater honour by our dress and that this is also God's intention. It is also interesting that, as in Mark 10, we find no emphasis given here to marriage or sexual intercourse as valid only or even primarily for the sake of bearing children. As Gundry-Volf observes, 'Paul sees the *lovers* Adam and Eve as Christians' prototypes, but not *father* Adam and *mother* Eve.'[40] 'Paul's silence about procreation as the purpose of Christian marriage is telling, given the Jewish view of marriage as an obligation for the sake of producing children, a view we might expect Paul to espouse.'[41]

One can read Paul as seeing marriage as a necessary evil, a second best to celibacy, 'only as a necessity, a solution to a particular problem,'[42] and therefore demeaning of marriage and sexuality. To some degree this is true, but Paul apparently cannot give up what he knows about creation and so does not condemn either marriage or sexual desire. Indeed he urges that partners – reflecting a striking mutuality in his view of marriage – should give each other their sexual rights and that each has authority over the other in this (1 Cor. 7.3–4). Here, too, Paul falls somewhat short of the affirmation of sexual intimacy implied in Jesus' argument. Putting sexual intercourse into the context of rights creates a basis for potential abuse, including marital rape, though clearly that is not Paul's intent. On the positive side he is affirming the appropriateness of sexual desire and its expression and a fair reading would assume that in using the cold language of rights he means also that each respect the other's rights in a broader sense. Paul's notion of marriage as a defence against sexual immorality is not dissimilar to the argument in Sir. 36.34–37, which portrays upholding marriage as a fortification against potential ruin. The same affirmation of sexual desire runs through what appears to be Paul's reluctant defence against those wanting to make his own preferred position a rule for all. That reluctance shows in his urging people to remain celibate like himself, if they can (1 Cor. 7.8–9, 25–27, 36–39), but he is equally at pains to emphasize against the rigorists that those who feel they must give expression to their sexuality in marriage are not sinning (7.28). We shall return to the weighting Paul gives to celibacy and to the question of what status he gives to the statement, 'It is well for a man not to touch a woman,' in our discussion of celibacy in Chapter 6. In 1 Corinthians 7.7 he insists that both options, celibacy or marriage, are God's gift.

Marriage in household codes: Colossians

Marriages did not exist in isolation, but belonged to households, to which sometimes more than one married couple belonged and more than one generation, whether squatting in the squalor of a single room or in larger establishments which included slaves. Such larger settings are assumed in the instructions to household members found in Colossians 3.18—4.1 and their elaboration in Ephesians 5.21—6.9. These writings, and even more so the letters to Timothy and Titus, reflect a later situation than that of the undisputed letters of Paul, where the authors (or, some argue, the older Paul) no longer assume history will soon be brought to a close by Christ's coming, but need to offer instruction about what it means to take one's place in the world. As Balch has shown,[43] these stand in a tradition of practical instruction about households, about wives and husbands, slaves and masters, and children and fathers, which reaches back to Aristotle, and reflects the norms valued in society. We find the pattern in Pseudo-Phocylides, where it is assumed as a way of addressing what is also right order according to God's law (175–227).

In Colossians the instructions to marriage partners are brief: 'Wives, be subject to your husbands, as is fitting in the Lord. Husbands, love your wives and never treat them harshly' (3.18–19). Neither Jews nor Gentiles would find anything surprising in the hierarchy this assumes, because it was the common view. As noted in the previous chapter, for a man to play a woman's role was shameful because it lowered his status, and for a woman to reverse roles was seen as an offence. There were strong women, such as the hero Judith, who, as a widow, ran her own estate, but they were exceptions which proved the rule. As Beattie observes, 'such apparent conservatism does not derive from any great love for the world, but rather from the need to survive in uncongenial surroundings until Christ is revealed'.[44] It may, as Winter suggests, also serve to address concerns in the wider community about the movement among elite Roman women, who were asserting their rights to greater power and influence and flouting conventions, by ensuring no such impression could be gained of Christian women.[45] It is probably also formulated over against the rival interpreters of Paul who appear to have laid emphasis on celibacy, if that is what 'do not handle' and 'do not touch' mean in Colossians 2.21.[46] The author of 1 Timothy similarly appears to be resisting such a movement in 1 Timothy 4.3, when he speaks of people opposing marriage. At the same time women's place in the hierarchy included considerable exercise of power as the usual managers of the domestic household, which would have included significant status when they played host to Christian communities in their household, such as Nympha did in Laodicea (Col. 4.15–16).[47] To describe something as being 'fitting in the Lord' may be connecting normal social practice with divine will, assumed as proper order, perhaps also reflecting a particular interpretation of Genesis, to which we return in our discussion of 1 Corinthians 11 below. The author is certainly aware of the potential for abuse in such an unequal relationship, where the man had power, usually including physical power, but infuses the structure with Christian love, though love of one's spouse was a common theme of the day also in Jewish and especially Graeco-Roman literature.[48] Marriage here, unlike in 1 Corinthians 7, is no longer primarily a strategy for channelling dangerous passions, but a normal state of existence.[49]

Marriage and household codes: Ephesians

In the elaboration of this instruction in Ephesians we find the Christian element greatly expanded. It begins: 'Be subject to one another out of reverence for Christ' (5.21). The mutuality is striking as is its problematic nature, since it might engender a downward spiral of mutual submission until one wonders when it should stop and decisions could be made. The author clearly does not intend that nor intend consensus, but assumes a kind of mutuality still governed by the hierarchy of men over women. Accordingly, he does not follow 'Wives, be subject to your husbands' by 'Husbands, be subject to your wives'. However, he adds the significant qualification: 'as you are to the Lord'. This might just mean: completely! But it has the effect of linking the woman's response to her husband to her response to the

Lord in a way that means they need to cohere – but leaves open how. The author reinforces the hierarchy with the words: 'For the husband is the head of the wife just as Christ is the head of the church, the body of which he is the Savior. Just as the church is subject to Christ, so also wives ought to be, in everything, to their husbands' (5.23–24). The context shows that *kephalē*, 'head', which in other contexts can mean 'source', indicates authority here.[50] Nevertheless by setting up the parallel between the husband and Christ as Saviour of the Church, the author effectively implies that the husband needs to act in the same way toward his wife as Christ does for the Church, which is clearly loving and not violent or exploitative. The instruction to husbands makes this clear:

> Husbands, love your wives, just as Christ loved the church and gave himself up for her, in order to make her holy by cleansing her with the washing of water by the word, so as to present the church to himself in splendor, without a spot or wrinkle or anything of the kind – yes, so that she may be holy and without blemish.
>
> (Eph. 5.25–27)

Here the author alludes to an element in wedding preparation, the washing of the bride, and reflects popular notions of what might add to a bride's attractiveness: 'without a spot or wrinkle or anything of the kind', imagery drawn from Ezekiel 16.8–14. He then applies the analogy:

> In the same way, husbands should love their wives as they do their own bodies. He who loves his wife loves himself. For no one ever hates his own body, but he nourishes and tenderly cares for it, just as Christ does for the church, because we are members of his body.
>
> (Eph. 5.28–30)

The allusion to bodily attractiveness in speaking of the Church fits the allusion here to bodies. This is a version of the golden rule: love your neighbour as you love yourself (Lev. 19.18). It does not say: 'do not love yourself, but only your wife', because on the author's assumptions the gospel is about love all around, so that husbands need to love their wives as well as they do themselves. Sexual union is part of loving. This is brought to focus very clearly in a passage in *Testament of Naphtali* 8.8–9, where the author applies loving one's neighbour to loving one's wife through sexual intercourse, but, in a manner not unlike Paul in 1 Corinthians 7.5, insists that it take second place to the greatest commandment to love God. At this point the author of Ephesians cites Genesis 2.24:

> 'For this reason a man will leave his father and mother and be joined to his wife, and the two will become one flesh.' This is a great mystery, and I am applying it to Christ and the church.   (Eph. 5.31–32)

The 'great mystery' appears to interpret the strange statement in Genesis 2.24 that two become one and, as the author indicates, to apply it to Christ and the Church being one. As earlier in the letter 'mystery' indicates God's plan, now revealed in Christ (Eph. 1.9; 3.3; 4.9; 6.19). Sexual union, implied in Genesis 2.24, is a widespread metaphor in many cultures for people's relation to the divine. It is implied already in Paul's rejection of believers engaging with a prostitute on grounds that they have been joined instead to Christ (1 Cor. 6.12–20). The unequal partnership is reflected in the author's conclusion: 'Each of you, however, should love his wife as himself, and a wife should respect (fear) her husband' (Eph. 5.33) and reinforced through the analogy which parallels the unequal relationship of Christ and the Church with husband and wife.[51] Here, as in Colossians, the author will be concerned about how the wider world reads Christianity as they see domestic behaviour,[52] especially of women, while at the same time embedding these instructions within a broader context which depicts the wider community as alien and hostile,[53] and an immediate context concerned with wise behaviour.[54]

Marriage and household codes: 1 Peter and Titus

We find related instructions given to wives and husbands in 1 Peter 3.1–7. After urging slaves to put up with suffering from their masters, the author adds:

> Wives, in the same way, accept the authority of your husbands, so that, even if some of them do not obey the word, they may be won over without a word by their wives' conduct, when they see the purity and reverence of your lives.   (1 Pet. 3.1–2)

'In the same way' should not be pressed, as though wives in relation to husbands are being equated with slaves in relation to masters. The language of subordination is the same as in Colossians and Ephesians, 'be subject', but translated differently here as 'accept the authority of'. It indicates the common hierarchy. The passage addresses also the possibility of mixed marriages and assumes their validity as did Paul in 1 Corinthians 7. These would have posed serious problems, because as Collins notes, proselytes, for instance, were expected to sever all previous family ties, and Plutarch (a second-century CE Greek moral philosopher) says a wife should worship the gods of her husband (*Moralia* 140D).[55]

The author then imposes restrictions:

> Do not adorn yourselves outwardly by braiding your hair, and by wearing gold ornaments or fine clothing; rather, let your adornment be the inner self with the lasting beauty of a gentle and quiet spirit, which is very precious in God's sight. It was in this way long ago that the holy women who hoped in God used to adorn themselves by accepting the authority of their husbands. Thus Sarah obeyed Abraham and called him lord. You have become her daughters as long as you do what is good and never let fears alarm you.   (1 Pet. 3.3–6)

The negative approach to braided hair, gold ornaments and fine clothing stands in contrast to the images of the holy city adorned as a bride for her husband (cf. Rev. 20.2). The author offers no reason except to offer a better option: 'the lasting beauty of a gentle and quiet spirit', which as with the slaves would not 'rock the boat', and cites what he sees as Sarah's submission to Abraham as a model. Like the ordered hierarchy of household life, modesty of apparel was a common theme in the wider society, where excess and ornamentation were taken as signs of loose behaviour.[56] They should do good and not fear, which assumes there were fears to be suppressed, such as fear of persecution from the authorities; for well-behaved households do not attract suspicion. The instruction to husbands is brief: 'Husbands, in the same way, show consideration for your wives in your life together, paying honor to the woman as the weaker sex (lit. 'vessel'), since they too are also heirs of the gracious gift of life – so that nothing may hinder your prayers' (1 Pet. 3.7). It acknowledges inequality in describing women as the weaker vessels, a term used of physical bodies. They are to be honoured as fellow recipients of the gift of life, presumably the gospel. The notion that wrongdoing might impair the effectiveness of prayers was widespread.

The concern that wives live in submission to their husbands finds expression also in Titus 2.4–5, where older women are told to instruct younger ones 'to love their husbands, to love their children, to be self-controlled, chaste, good managers of the household, kind, being submissive to their husbands, so that the word of God may not be discredited'. Winter suggests this may reflect alleged assertions about Cretan lifestyle as neglectful of household and marriage (cf. 1.5).[57] We also find instructions that slaves be told 'to be submissive to their masters and to give satisfaction in every respect; they are not to talk back, not to pilfer, but to show complete and perfect fidelity, so that in everything they may be an ornament to the doctrine of God our Savior' (2.9–10), but as in 1 Peter without matching instructions for masters.

Slaves and sex

If we return to the household instruction in Colossians and Ephesians we find the author addressing parents (especially fathers) and children, and slaves and masters. Both 1 Peter 2.18–25 and Titus 2.9–10, just cited, address slaves, but not masters. In none of the instructions to slaves do sexual themes appear, but the silence is surprising and difficult to interpret, given the prevalence of sexual exploitation of slaves, seen by many as a right.[58] Biblical provisions which forbid sex with someone else's slave (Lev. 19.20; see also 4QD^e/4Q270 4 13–19) appear to assume it, though Ben Sira forbade it (41.22 manuscript M). Stories of Abraham and Jacob, who slept with their wives' slaves, appear to reflect the assumption that it was acceptable. As Osiek observes, 'The lingering question with regard to sexual abuse is whether or not, contrary to accepted custom, Christian teachers would have thought from the earliest years that making use of the sexual availability of one's slaves was abusive and wrong,'[59] though not all such relations would have been experienced as abusive.[60] The situation would have been acute for slaves with non-believing masters. The author of 1 Peter makes mention of the potential for grave suffering, likening it to Christ's (2.18–25), but is not explicit. We can only speculate that the instruction to masters in Colossians and Ephesians that they treat slaves fairly and remember they must account for themselves before their heavenly Master would have implied that sexual exploitation was forbidden, but we cannot know for sure. Certainly the kind of treatment encouraged by Paul in his letter to Philemon about the runaway slave Onesimus would indicate that such abuse would be out of the question.

Women in worship: 1 Timothy 2.8–15

The forbidding of adornment in 1 Peter 3.3 finds an echo in 1 Timothy 2.8–10, where again the beauty of inner piety is preferred.

> I desire, then, that in every place the men should pray, lifting up holy hands without anger or argument; also that the women should dress themselves modestly and decently in suitable clothing, not with their hair braided, or with gold, pearls, or expensive clothes, but with good works, as is proper for women who profess reverence for God.
>
> (1 Tim. 2.8–10)

The context here, however, appears to be gatherings for prayer, presumably community worship. In this setting we also find restrictions imposed on women:

> Let a woman learn in silence with full submission. I permit no woman to teach or to have authority over a man; she is to keep silent. For Adam was formed first, then Eve; and Adam was not deceived, but the woman was deceived and became a transgressor. Yet she will be saved through childbearing, provided they continue in faith and love and holiness, with modesty.
>
> (1 Tim. 2.11–15)

Gynē, 'woman', could be translated 'wife' and *anēr*, 'man', as 'husband'. If specifically addressing married couples it asserts the wife's submission to her husband, consistent with the other texts we have considered. The reference to anger and argument in 2.8 may indicate a concern in addition with conflict between the two in the context of worship. The author more probably intends this to apply to all women present, as he does the instruction about modesty. Adam and Eve represent more than only husbands and wives. The grounds indicated for asserting the requirement of submission here derive not from cultural norms, with which they are in harmony and to which they are doubtless sensitive, but from Genesis. The man has the superior position because (a) Adam was made before Eve; (b) Eve was deceived and became the transgressor, not Adam. The author almost gives the impression that Adam, himself, did not sin, but only Eve, and perhaps intended this. Certainly what follows gives the impression that only she (and so all women after her) has a problem, not Adam (and men). It reflects an exegetical tradition (*Life of Adam and Eve* 18.1; *Apocalypse of Moses* 14.2; probably already in Sir. 25.24) which assumes Eve was sexually seduced, an interpretation made possible by the Greek of Genesis 3.13 which uses a word which can mean seduce as well as just deceive and which we see already influencing Paul in 2 Corinthians 11.2–3.

The author's assurance about women in 2.15 derives from an understanding of God's declaration to the woman in Genesis 3.16 that she (and all women after her) would endure pain in childbearing. It understands this as paying the penalty for her deed. The words, 'she shall be saved through childbearing', have evoked a range of explanations from being saved in some physical way in the process of childbearing to being saved as a result of Eve's descendant giving birth to the Messiah.[61] They might still be interpreting Genesis 3.16, which in its Greek translation refers to the woman constantly returning to her husband and his ruling over her. On this reading that would 'save' her in the sense of giving her security. Winter suggests it means saving her from having an abortion with all its concomitant dangers at that time.[62] Fiore suggests it may reflect the merits of engagement in procreation, a major emphasis in moral philosophy of the time.[63] In addition, however, women need also to 'continue in faith and love and holiness, with modesty', the author, typically of those trained in rhetoric, returning to the theme with which he began in 2.9–10, modest attire. The restriction on women with regard to teaching and giving verbal response in learning or making any comment at all is closely related to what we find in 1 Corinthians 14.33b–36. Let us now explore this further.

Women in worship: 1 Corinthians 14.33b–36

The issue of women's place in worship arises in two different settings in 1 Corinthians. In 14.33b–36 we read:

> As in all the churches of the saints, women should be silent in the churches. For they are not permitted to speak, but should be subordinate, as the law also says. If there is anything they desire to know, let them ask their husbands at home. For it is shameful for a woman to speak in church. Or did the word of God originate with you? Or are you the only ones it has reached?　　　　(1 Cor. 14.33b–36)

Some manuscripts (D, F, G) relocate its key statements in 14.34–35 to the end of the chapter. Its textual instability, together with its perceived tension with 11.2–16 and other indicators of women's leadership roles in worship, its awkwardness in its setting, its distinctive language and use of the law, and its closeness to the later 1 Timothy 2.11–12, have suggested to some that it is not original to this context but has been added by a later hand.[64] Collins suggests that Paul may be citing a ruling in 14.34–35 only to challenge it in 14.36.[65] Økland rightly resists this conclusion, arguing that no manuscript omits it, and that its ideas cohere with Paul's stance elsewhere.[66] If taken as authentically part of Paul's letter, then we need to explain how Paul here silences women whereas 11.2–16 assumes they speak. Wire suggests a development in Paul's argument that begins with some tolerance and ends with none, with which Beattie concurs, pointing also to Paul's appeal to the law in 1 Corinthians 7.19; 9.8.[67] On the basis of noting that *gynaikes*, translated 'women' here, can also have the narrow meaning, 'wives', Schüssler Fiorenza suggested that this passage refers only to wives, whereas 11.2–16 refers to celibate women and widows.[68] Against this, as Økland notes, Paul's argument in 11.2–16 speaks of women generally, including women as giving birth, so must have all women in mind.[69] She then suggests that the difference between the two passages relates to roles: in the ancient Mediterranean 'female "prophets" were generally accepted, where female teachers were generally banned'.[70] Accordingly 11.2–16 affirms the former, whereas 14.33b–36 prohibits the latter. She sees the reference to questions and answers as reflecting common teaching techniques of the day.[71] Winter notes that Roman law prevented women from intervening on behalf of their husbands in the context of legal argument.[72] Nothing in the context suggests that simple chatter was a problem. The language of shame reflects the common concerns about honour and shame. A wife engaging in teaching in her husband's presence might be seen as taking a male role, an issue of sensitivity detected also behind Romans 1.

Women in worship: 1 Corinthians 11.2–16

Paul begins and ends his discussion of women's attire in worship in 1 Corinthians 11.2–16 by appealing to established tradition, praising and then urging conformity. In between he argues why such attire matters. He begins in 11.3 by identifying a sequence: God–Christ–man–woman, using *kephalē*, commonly translated 'head', which fits the context about head covering, but which could also be understood as 'source', suggested by the references to creation and origins in 11.8–9. In any case, as Økland notes, 'source' would still imply hierarchy on the basis of the common belief that in such matters what is prior in time is prior in value.[73] In 11.4 Paul then clearly refers to a man's head, declaring it shameful for him to prophesy or pray with it covered and in 11.5 states the reverse for a woman: shame if she is not covered. Paul may also be concerned about men's behaviour, as Winter suggests,[74] but he is certainly concerned primarily with women's. He then explains that he sees a woman having her head uncovered as the equivalent of having it shaved (11.6), something done to humjliate immoral women, as everyone knew, which then brought disgrace on both them and their husbands. Not all hearers would have accepted the analogy.

Paul extends the argument, declaring on the basis of his reading of his Greek version of Genesis 1—2, that man is the image and glory of God and woman is the glory of man, a hierarchy of being (11.7–8). The argument for male superiority continues in 11.9 where on the basis of Genesis he argues that the man was not made for woman but woman for man. In 11.10 Paul slips in a further argument, based on the belief that in worship angels are present, which may have two implications. First, one should not expose oneself shamefully before them since, it is assumed, they are present in worship, a view reflected in texts from Qumran (1QM/1Q33 7.4–6; 1QSa/1Q28a 2.3–11), and, second, one should also not tempt them, possibly in allusion to the myth of the lustful angels of Genesis 6.1–4 and *1 Enoch* 6—16.[75] Martin argues that the veil then as the veil in many cultures today is to be seen as relating to sex, and so here in relation to men present as both protecting women from their gaze and protecting men from their sexual attractiveness.[76] Winter interprets 'angels' differently, noting that the Greek word can also mean 'messengers' and so might refer to people spying to see if this new Christian movement is another instance of the widespread sexual laxity characteristic of the elite women's movement spreading from Rome through the empire.[77] Removing the veil would be read as denying your husband's authority and so tantamount to adultery.[78]

In 11.11–12 Paul steps back from what might easily have seemed like a denigration of women. That was not his intention at all; it was just the issue of attire. So he asserts that both women and men belong together (11.11) and with playful acumen points out that, yes, woman was created from man, but all men were born from women (11.12)! Affirming both men and women had been the focus of Galatians 3.28, which in allusion to Genesis 1.27 spoke of 'male and female' being one in Christ, besides slave and free, Jew and Greek, without denying their differences. Some read Paul's discussion in 1 Corinthians 11 as contradicting what they see as the radical equality of Galatians 3.28. Alternatively, we can see 1 Corinthians 11 as indicative of how Paul would have understood Galatians 3.28, namely not as non-hierarchical, but as implying that oneness exists among all, despite both their differences and their station.[79] Meeks noted that behind Galatians 3.28 may lie the myth of androgyny, that is, of return to the ideal of human being that is neither male nor female,[80] but others have pointed out that where such images of androgyny do exist they usually assume a return of all to a male form.[81] Another proposal is that Galatians 3.28 alludes not only to Genesis 1.27 but also to Genesis 2.24, so that here becoming one employs the analogy of marriage as in Ephesians 5.31–32 and 2 Corinthians 11.2–3 (implied also in 1 Cor. 6.17), which some might then use as a basis for arguing abandonment of marriage.[82] Perhaps the absence of 'male and female' from the parallel statement to Galatians 3.28 which appears in 1 Corinthians 12.13 reflects Paul's concerns that the text may encourage the kind of denial of sexuality he is having to combat at Corinth.

Having made his pitch for a limited equality, Paul resorts to what he sees as nevertheless proper and natural differences which should not be obliterated. Of course – he assumes the Corinthians would agree – long hair on a man is degrading (because it makes him look like a woman, a humiliating downgrade), but long hair on a woman is her glory (11.14–15; similarly Pseudo-Phocylides 212). For Paul all these reasons cohere, so that 'natural' here is not mere convention as we might see it but the way God made things to be. As in Romans 1 various value systems merge, combining what most Greeks (in contrast to Jews and Romans) would have also said[83] with what Paul saw mandated in his Greek Old Testament, that woman is the image of man as man is the image of God and then naturally this had to be expressed by how one covered or uncovered the head. On the considerable discussion about whether Paul is referring to hairstyle or head covering see the discussions in Collins and Thiselton.[84]

As Økland notes, the issue is not primarily women's subordination, otherwise Paul would have no need to mention men's appearance, but gender boundaries.[85] These both had the effect of constituting worship as predominantly male space, and of creating, nevertheless, a framework which enabled women to operate within it.[86]

Women and men in leadership

Depending on how one resolves the relation between 14.34–35 and 11.2–16, Paul either decided in the end to silence all women in gatherings for worship, or allowed them defined roles (prayer or prophecy but not teaching), or in tension with the former affirmed their exercising the same roles as men in ministry provided they attired themselves as nature and creation required. Certainly Paul assumes that women exercised leadership in ministry as Romans 16 indicates (see also Phil. 4.2–3; Col. 4.14). Was Prisca really to keep silent or refrain from teaching when Prisca and Aquila appeared together (Rom. 16.3; cf. Acts 18.26)? One might ask the same of Andronicus and Junia or Philogus and Julia (Rom. 16.7, 15).[87]

Certainly Paul seems aware of the need to affirm the place of women and men together in the community of faith. In this he stands in a tradition evident in the anecdotes about Jesus, who, despite appointing an all-male inner band, similarly affirmed women's place. As we shall see in the next chapter, Jesus places the responsibility on men for what they do with their sexuality and does not blame women for men's actions or depict women as dangerous or evil and so needing to be avoided or controlled. This helps explain the openness to inclusion of women, such as those who according to Mark 15.40–44 travelled with him from Galilee to Jerusalem or those whom Luke portrays as among his supporters, including Joanna, a spouse of one of Antipas' officials. Jesus engaged with women, sometimes in contexts of healing (Mark 1.29–31; 5.21–43; 7.24–30; Luke 7.11–17), and on one occasion with an openness which apparently surprised and shocked other men present, for he responded to the woman who anointed his feet not as if in danger and needing to maintain distance and control, but generously and non-exploitively (Luke 7.36–50), an element common to all versions of the story (see Mark 14.3–9; Matt. 26.6–13; John 12.1–8).[88] All make her a model of true faith, most dramatically reflected in John 13.11–17, where Jesus himself washes his disciples' feet and bids them do the same. John 4.27 reports the same sense of surprise at Jesus' open encounter with the Samaritan woman. Both women and men feature significantly in Jesus' parables, though mostly in traditional roles. In the first three Gospels it is notably women who stand with him to the end, though at a distance, while the men flee, and all four depict women as key witnesses to his resurrection (Mark 16.1–8; Matt. 28.1–10; Luke 24.1–9; John 20.1–18). As we shall see in Chapter 6, sometimes Jesus clashed with the traditional expectations of household and family – including his own, according to Mark, when Mary wanted him home and he responded by declaring a new family entity consisting of the faithful around him (3.20–21, 30–35).

There is sufficient evidence from a diverse range of anecdotes to indicate that Jesus did not view women as dangerous because of their sexuality, but engaged them with the same openness he did men. This had the potential to challenge normal social expectations of gender roles, and apparently on occasion it did, especially when they clashed with his insistence on a higher loyalty to God's agenda of the kingdom, but otherwise he expressed his openness still within the broad cultural and religious framework of his day, which probably accounts for his choice of twelve men as leaders of his renewed Israel. This does not exclude the possibility that the women who were also among the wider group of disciples will have exercised a leadership role. This would make good sense of their appearance as leaders in Paul's letters, where having female as well as male leaders seemed not to be an issue, and their mention was quite incidental, as part of what Paul obviously considered normal and not requiring any particular justification. In time the tension between broad cultural and religious norms and the new gospel openness, reflected in Jesus' choice of the twelve and then Paul's concern with attire, would be resolved more in favour of the former.

4

Adultery, attitude and disorder

In this chapter we consider passages in the NT which depict what the authors see as sexual wrongdoing. Already in Chapter 2 we considered one instance. Here we consider the rest. We begin with adultery.

Adultery

Disapproval of adultery was standard both in biblical and Jewish circles (Exod. 20.14; Deut. 5.18) and also in Greek and Roman culture.[1] Adultery entailed a man having sexual intercourse with another man's wife. It is to be distinguished from having intercourse, for instance, with a prostitute, unless she was married, or with an unmarried woman, including a widow or divorcee. Within the social framework of households at the head of which was normally a male, adultery was a form of theft by one man of what belonged to another man and complicity in theft by that man's wife. Subverting a marriage by adultery, therefore, had the potential to undermine the wider family or clan and its interests. It threatened the production of offspring who were necessary for the family's future stability and wealth. Biblical law required the execution of both parties (Lev. 20.10; Deut. 22.22), though it is unclear to what extent this was carried out in the first century, when Jewish authorities lacked the authority to do so. On the other hand the story attached to John 7 in some manuscripts might indicate that mobs could still take the law into their own hands (7.53—8.11).

Adultery was rarely depicted as wronging a woman or as emotional hurt to either partner, though where emphasis lay on mutual love, as in popular romantic literature of the Roman period, this was more likely to occur. Perhaps the strongest emotional responses to adultery are found in the symbolic use of adultery to depict Israel's waywardness in turning aside to idols from God, where God's jealous anger and vengeance are declared, as in Ezekiel 16, though from the perspective of offended honour rather than any depiction of personal hurt.[2] The symbolic application of adultery in this way lives on in references to the adulterous and sinful generation of Jesus' time (Mark 8.38; Matt. 12.39; 16.4), to adulterous friendship with the world (James 4.4), and to following the prophet Jezebel (Rev. 2.22).

The NT displays an unquestioning espousal of the Ten Commandments, including the prohibition of adultery. Sometimes it is cited without particular emphasis alongside the commandments not to murder and to steal, such as in Jesus' response to the rich man's quest for eternal life according to Mark 10.19 (Matt. 19.18; Luke 18.20), in Paul's summary of the law in Romans 13.9 (similarly 2.22), and in James 2.11. The word, adultery, appears in many of the lists which we consider below, including in the prayer of the proud Pharisee (Luke 18.11). In the next chapter we shall see how most of the sayings attributed to Jesus about divorce speak of remarriage as adultery on the assumption that the first marriage remains intact. Adultery also came into play during the period of betrothal, so that when Joseph learns that Mary is pregnant, he assumes that she had committed adultery with someone (Matt. 1.18–19). He further assumes that because of it his marriage to her is at an end. This understanding is widely attested and probably has its roots in Deuteronomy 24.1–4, according to which a man may not receive back his original wife even after he has legitimately divorced her and she has legitimately remarried, and then been divorced again or widowed, because she has become unclean for him. Similarly *Jubilees* shows Jacob never again engaging in sexual intercourse with Bilhah after she was raped by Reuben, because she had been rendered thereby unclean for him (33.9; similarly *Test. Reuben* 3.15). This understanding was enshrined also in Roman law, which required dissolution of marriages where adultery had taken place,[3] and survived to some degree until the twentieth century in many jurisdictions where adultery was considered as automatic ground for divorce, though not requiring it. We may suspect that many marriages still persisted after adultery in the world of the NT, but it was not the official option and, Matthew assumes, not one which Joseph considered as he planned to end the betrothal/marriage privately. Joseph is deemed righteous (1.19) because he chose the more compassionate of the two options before him, namely, public or private divorce. Continuing the marriage was not an option.

Adultery and attitude

The most direct discussion of adultery comes in the so-called Sermon on the Mount of Matthew's Gospel, where, probably drawing on an already expanded version of a collection of Jesus' sayings attested also in Luke 6.20–49, Matthew presents a block of Jesus' teaching to commence his account of Jesus' ministry (5.1—7.28). With echoes of Moses on Mount Sinai, Jesus sits on a mountain and, having announced future blessings to the needy and faithful (5.3–12), declares that he has come not to set the law aside but to fulfil it (5.17–20). After that declaration of intent, Matthew has Jesus present a sixfold exposition of what Jesus' statement means, carefully crafted into two groups of three, a favourite structural device in Matthew, and introduced with the words, 'You have heard that it was said', followed by, 'but I say' (5.21–48). They cover murder, adultery, divorce, oaths, retaliation, and love of enemies.

Some read this as Jesus presenting a new law to replace the old. This entails a reading of the statement of intent in 5.17 along the lines that Jesus came not to abolish the law and the prophets, but to fulfil the latter's promise of something new and to fulfil the former by replacing it with something better, perhaps also seeing this as fulfilling the old's intent.[4] The next statement about not a jot or stroke falling from the law (5.18) would describe the existing law's authority, but only up to the time of its fulfilment and replacement by Jesus. The following statement about those who set aside even the least part of the law (5.19) would then refer to the new law, and the final statement about exceeding the righteousness of the scribes and Pharisees (5.20) would be declaring what is now possible on the basis of the new law of Jesus.[5] The six contrasts which follow set the new law over against the old law.

Others read 5.17 as Jesus declaring, against accusers or/and believers who might think otherwise, that he did not come to abolish or set aside the law and the prophets, but to fulfil them in the sense of doing what they declare should be done and will be done.[6] They read the next statement about jots and strokes (5.18) as reinforcing this continuing validity of the law, and the following statement (5.19) as threatening exclusion against any teaching otherwise. The final statement (5.20) insists on a better level of performance in keeping the law than that of the scribes and Pharisees. They read the six contrasts not as playing off a new law against the old, but as contrasting how people were hearing and applying the law with what it really meant.[7]

Whereas those stressing discontinuity point to the law on divorce and oaths as setting aside the old law,[8] those emphasizing continuity point out that Jesus' approach here is not atypical of what other Jewish teachers had done in sharpening and radicalizing the existing law, which might include in the process some setting aside of laws.[9] The author of the *Temple Scroll* clearly champions the law while at the same time imposing some requirements that went beyond it and by implication set some things aside, such as polygyny for kings (57.15–18), which the *Damascus Document* demands of all (4.20–1). Enhancing the law's strictness or refusing to do what it permits is not abrogation. Such authors saw themselves not as setting the law aside but as upholding and enhancing it. Such is probably also Matthew's view.[10]

The issue has been debated not only in relation to this passage but also in relation to the historical Jesus and his attitude towards the law. In the so-called second quest of the historical Jesus which flourished in the mid-twentieth century, it was common to cite Jesus' teaching on oaths and divorce as evidence that Jesus set law aside in favour of the principle of love.[11] This entailed attributing the sayings about the law's permanence to conservative Jewish Christian circles wanting to reverse Jesus' approach. Such an understanding of the historical Jesus has potentially far-reaching implications for weighing how he might have approached biblical commandments pertaining to sex, including same-sex relations, and has been used to suggest that he might well have set them aside.[12] More recent studies have recognized that the image of Jesus as law observant and promoting law observance is reflected not only in Matthew and Luke (Matt. 5.18; Luke 16.17; Matt. 23.23; Luke 11.42), but also deeply rooted in their common source Q and historically more plausible. The conflicts reported in the earliest traditions between Jesus and his contemporaries related not to the validity of biblical law but to its interpretation and where the emphasis should lie. Depictions of his trial give no hint that people heard Jesus as rejecting the law.

Much of the evidence points to Jesus as having had a fairly conservative approach, illustrated by his initially hesitant response to the request of the Syro-Phoenician woman in Mark 7.24–30[13] and his identification with John the Baptist's very strict espousal of Leviticus 18.16; 20.21 in condemning Herod's marriage to the wife of his half-brother (Mark 6.17–18). As Meier observes, 'Perhaps one reason that we have so little from the historical Jesus on sexual topics is that, apart from the two special cases of divorce and celibacy, where he diverged from mainstream Judaism, his views were those of mainstream Judaism.'[14] Socially and culturally it would have, so to speak, stood out like a sore thumb to his contemporaries, had he defied the law. Jesus' conflicts were above all over such issues as whether the requirement to exercise compassion and healing overrode the requirement to observe Sabbath, what in such circumstances counted as a breach, and whether reaching out to sinners should carry more weight than observing laws concerned to protect one's ritual or moral purity, where they clashed. Typical of Jesus' approach was the declaration that the Sabbath was made for people, not people for the Sabbath (Mark 2.27), and his defending his stance through parables which expounded love and compassion as paramount. The step beyond setting priorities to setting laws aside, such as circumcision, came later where new circumstances demanded that some laws be permanently overridden. That caused huge controversy, and the diverse stances have left some trace in the writings of the NT. Matthew and Luke preserve the stance closer in substance to that of Jesus (Luke sanctioning minimal change: circumcision of Gentile converts). Paul and Mark reflect more thoroughgoing change, which some claim matched better the spirit of Jesus' priorities.[15]

Matthew's more cautious approach is the setting for development of the six contrasts in 5.21–48. In at least the first two there is no debate that both enhance what the law commands. In the first the focus shifts from murder to hate, identified here as hate-filled anger, which it illustrates as also expressing itself in hateful name-calling (5.21–22). The upshot is that taking this commandment seriously means not harbouring attitudes of hate toward anyone, even if, as the next illustration indicates, it means travelling back up from Jerusalem to Galilee to seek reconciliation before sacrificing at the Temple (5.23–24). The first and last contrasts thus follow a similar theme, the last emphasizing love of one's enemy (5.43–48). This brings us to the second contrast.

> You have heard that it was said, 'You shall not commit adultery.' But I say to you that everyone who looks at a woman with lust has already committed adultery with her in his heart. (5.27–28)

The NRSV translators have already made some decisions about the meaning of the original Greek which we must reconsider. The first is *gynē* translated 'woman', which in Greek also means 'wife'. Whichever translation we choose, the reference is clearly to someone else's wife, for that is what constitutes adultery. It may imply that the same principle applies to relations with other women,[16] but that is not what the text is addressing here. Much more complicated is the issue surrounding the words translated 'with lust'. A very literal translation would read either: 'with a view to desiring her' or 'with the result that he desires her'. Both translations are possible. The latter, widely held in the early Church, could then be taken to mean that any man who looks at another man's wife and as a result lusts after her or even finds himself sexually aroused by her or finds her sexually attractive commits adultery.[17] The consequences which might flow from this include that one could see just having sexual responses, whether acted on or not, as evil (except when they are to one's own wife) and that one would see other men's wives as therefore a constant threat because they might evoke such responses. When the Vulgate translation uses the word *mulier*, 'woman' not 'wife', then potentially looking at any women except one's wife is dangerous. Such readings make sense of strategies to make sure women are covered up to save men from this predicament. At worst they lead to the situation where women are held responsible for men's sexual responses. It comes close to this in the *Testament of Reuben*, which claims angelic revelation for its belief that women suffer a sickness (6.3) in that they have less ability than men to control their sexual desires (5.3), were to blame for seducing the Watchers (5.6–7) and conquering kings (*Test. Judah* 15.5–6) and pose a constant threat to men (3.10; 4.1).

It is also possible to translate the phrase as 'with the result that she desires',[18] but this does not fit well the words which follow: 'in his heart'. Elsewhere in Matthew the same Greek phrase occurs with the meaning not 'as a result of' but 'for the purpose of' (6.1; 23.5). This is the more likely meaning here, so that the issue is intent.[19] Thus whoever looks at someone else's wife with a view to lusting after her is well on the way to adultery whether the result is action or not. The saying goes further than that. It declares: such a response *is* adultery 'in his heart', that is, in his mind, and so should be included when we hear the command, not to commit adultery, just as hateful anger should be in the commandment about murder. These shifts are

important because they also reflect a shift from what can be prose-
cuted in a court of law, murder and adultery, to how we relate to one
another, where attitudes matter, not just actions.

Focusing just on actions is very limiting and according to Jesus
fails the commandments' intent. This is already apparent in the last
of the Ten Commandments, usually translated by the rarely used
word 'covet'. The Greek version uses the word for desire, meaning
desire with a view to wanting to have what is not yours. It is therefore
directly relevant to the exposition of Jesus here, since beside com-
manding people not to want to have their neighbour's house or male
or female slave or animal, it declares they are not to want to have
their neighbour's wife (Exod. 20.17). In fact the version in Deuteronomy
5.21 makes desiring your neighbour's wife a prohibition standing
on its own, followed by its Greek translator but also the translator
of Exodus. More than just greed, desire here evokes the power of
misdirected passion, a widely acknowledged danger in both Jewish
and Graeco-Roman literature of the time. These two prohibitions
(adultery and greed) are linked also in Pseudo-Philo 44.6–7, 10 and
4 Maccabees 2.4–6. People understood the eyes as a vehicle of both
greed and lust (e.g. Sir. 9.8; CD 2.16; 1QpHab 5.7–8; *Ps. Sol.* 4.11–12).
Warnings about adulterous looking and not just deeds were a common element in Jewish teaching (Sir. 9.8; Job 31.1; *Test. Reuben* 3.10;
Susanna 7–8), sometimes depicting women as dangerous, sometimes
blaming men, not women at all.

Thus Jesus shares with many Jewish authors of the time the view
that men are to take responsibility for their sexuality, not women,
and not seek to cover and control them. Jesus belongs with those
who do not see women as a danger or threat, though clearly not all
his disciples shared this stance. Some baulk at his speaking openly
with a woman in Samaria (John 4.27); they are, with others, taken
aback at his response to the woman who anointed him (Mark 14.3–9;
Luke 7.36–50), but find themselves in a mixed company of disciples,
which only a positive stance towards women would have made possible. Jesus resisted the flippant approach to women and sexuality,
expressed by some Sadducees in Mark 12.18–23. Matthew's genealogy
of Jesus, which gives special place to women deemed outsiders (1.1–
18), is well attuned to what was Jesus' own stance.

The connection to the exposition about murder (5.21–26) is
instructive for understanding how the author understands sexual

response. It is possible to read that exposition as outlawing anger altogether. One might then argue that he also outlaws all sexual responses. The latter is inherently unlikely, given the positive approach found elsewhere towards sexual desire and the focus on its control and direction. It is also unlikely that the author targets what we identify as anger, namely a common response associated with hurt and pain in us or others. Matthew happily depicts anger at wrongdoing as something positive in 18.35 (see also Mark 3.5). The exposition indicates a particular attitude embodying hatefulness towards others. In that sense it is likely that the issue of handling anger and sexual desire is the same. It is a matter of direction and intent. Anger is clearly to be brought under control by the overriding principle of love for the other, as the sixth matching contrast makes clear. Though not explicit, this principle should probably be seen as also informing the exposition of adultery. The expression 'commit adultery with her' does not imply 'against her' in Greek, though nor does it mean 'along with her'. It is best understood as 'in relation to her'.[20] The exposition of adultery, like that of murder, does have supplementary explanation, which raises even more issues. The explanation appears once more in Matthew in a different context, where it stands in parallel to Mark.

Cut it off!

In the context of the exposition of adultery, Matthew 5.29–30 must relate to sexual attitudes and behaviour. Possibly Matthew has adapted the saying he found in Mark, which he also brings in 18.8–9, although that cannot be proved (see the table opposite). The allusion to the 'right' eye and hand may indicate the saying's independent origin. Threat of hell (Gehenna, place of fiery punishment) matches the supplement to the exposition on murder in 5.22. That 5.29 first refers to the eye is appropriate, since the exposition has just spoken of seeing. The image of stumbling occurs elsewhere in warnings about sexual transgression (*Ps. Sol.* 16.8). Even more common is the connection between the eye and action in warnings about sexual wrongdoing (e.g. Sir. 9.8; 26.9; 41.20–21; *Jub.* 20.4; *Test. Reuben* 3.10). The allusion to the right eye probably reflects the general belief that the right side is more valuable. This adds to the drama of demanding that one pluck it out (Zech. 11.17; Josephus, *Antiquities* 6.69–72).[21] There is also widespread evidence in both Hellenistic and rabbinic literature

Table   The excision sayings in Mark and Matthew

Matthew 5.29–30	*Matthew 18.8–9*	*Mark 9.43–48*
(29) If your right eye causes you to sin, tear it out and throw it away; it is better for you to lose one of your members than for your whole body to be thrown into hell. (30) And if your right hand causes you to sin, cut it off and throw it away; it is better for you to lose one of your members than for your whole body to go into hell.	(8) If your hand or your foot causes you to stumble, cut it off and throw it away; it is better for you to enter life maimed or lame than to have two hands or two feet and to be thrown into the eternal fire. (9) And if your eye causes you to stumble, tear it out and throw it away; it is better for you to enter life with one eye than to have two eyes and to be thrown into the hell of fire.	(43) If your hand causes you to stumble, cut it off; it is better for you to enter life maimed than to have two hands and to go to hell, to the unquenchable fire. (44) (45) And if your foot causes you to stumble, cut it off; it is better for you to enter life lame than to have two feet and to be thrown into hell. (46) (47) And if your eye causes you to stumble, tear it out; it is better for you to enter the kingdom of God with one eye than to have two eyes and to be thrown into hell, (48) where their worm never dies, and the fire is never quenched.

for linking the cutting off of limbs with moral seriousness.[22] The value given the right hand in this saying has survived through to our own times – as a common prejudice of the right-handed! The hand might engage in adulterous behaviour in a variety of ways, touch being a vehicle of sexual expression. Some have suggested that the hand here might be a euphemism for the penis, as attested elsewhere (Isa. 56.2; 57.8; 1QS/1Q28 7.13), although the notion of the right hand makes this difficult. Others suggest that the author may be referring to masturbation, which later rabbinic literature describes as a sin of the hand, but again the right hand is an obstacle for this view, since then, and still in many cultures today, one handled one's genitals only with the left hand.[23] Most rightly see these demands not as something literal,[24] though such practices are known (Deut. 25.11–12 instructs that a woman's hands be cut off if in conflict she grabs a man's genitals),[25] but as illustrating the need for rigorous action.[26]

Notoriously the late second-century church father Origen took them literally and castrated himself.[27]

The sayings in Mark 9.43–48 follow another warning about stumbling: 'If any of you put a stumbling-block before one of these little ones who believe in me, it would be better for you if a great millstone were hung around your neck and you were thrown into the sea' (9.42). Even without the words 'in me' after 'believe', which some manuscripts lack, the phrase 'these little ones who believe' convinces many that the reference here is not to children,[28] but to believers.[29] The image of 'stumbling' could refer to any kind of sin or fall or it could refer to sexual wrongdoing. If the latter, then it refers either to causing another believer to sin sexually or causing a believing child to do so.[30] If the saying derives from the historical Jesus, it might have referred more generally to bringing harm to others or, in particular, to children. If understood in a sexual context it might at least include pederasty and through its dramatic formulation (being thrown to the bottom of the sea with a millstone round your neck!) might indicate particular abhorrence of such behaviour.[31] This is likely to be of particular relevance to Mark's hearers if living in Rome.[32]

The sayings in 9.43–48 may remain at the level of warnings to take all sin seriously and discipline oneself to avoid it. If, however, the focus of 9.42 already includes sexual sins, then it is possible that Matthew's application to sexual matters of the sayings similar to 9.43–48 may be consistent with their original import. Deming draws attention to later rabbinic traditions which speak not only of adultery of the hand, namely masturbation, but also of adultery in relation to the foot understood as euphemism for the penis. 'Foot' was an established euphemism for the penis (Exod. 4.25; Deut. 28.56; Isa. 6.2; 7.20; Ruth 3.4, 7, 8, 14). He speculates that this tradition, associated with first-century rabbis, may well be reflected in both Matthew 5.29–30 and Mark 9.43–48.[33] Alternatively the latter have influenced rabbinic tradition. It is therefore quite possible that Mark 9.43–48 targets sexual sin, adultery in particular, and 9.42 pederasty, but the issue can hardly be deemed certain. Given his use of the related sayings in 5.29–30, it is perhaps even more likely that Matthew intends such a reference in 18.6–9, but there we confront the same ambiguity about little ones (18.1–5), not least because Matthew adds material depicting them as beholding God's face (18.10) and clearly uses little ones elsewhere to refer to believers (10.41–42; 18.14; 25.31–48). Most, therefore, see no reference to pederasty, though a reading could be considered which saw it as a theme throughout, including as part of what might need to be confronted in church discipline in 18.15–20.[34]

Sexual wrongdoing and prostitution

In his exposition of the commandment not to commit adultery Philo of Alexandria draws together a number of other matters related to sexual wrongdoing (*Decalogue* 121).[35] Similarly Pseudo-Phocylides (3) and the early second-century Christian writing, the *Didache* (2.1–2) connect it with warnings against homoerotic behaviour. The commandment functions similarly as an umbrella in the NT. This probably accounts for the third contrast in Matthew's series of six, divorce. The list of evils in Mark 7.21–23 which flow from attitudes within, matching the emphasis in Matthew, shows similar signs of grouping. It lists two sets of three concepts matching the order of the commandments in Exodus 20.13–15 (adultery, theft, murder): sexual immorality–theft–murder and adultery–greed–wickedness.[36]

Some manuscripts of John's Gospel (and some of Luke) contain a famous anecdote about Jesus being confronted by a woman caught in adultery and her accusers (John 7.53—8.11). Nothing is said of the man involved. The issue is not approval or disapproval of the woman's deed, but what was an appropriate response. His words and enigmatic writing on the ground – whatever that meant – confronted the harshness and alleged hypocrisy of the accusers. He both instructs her not to sin again and sets her free to make a new beginning.

Adultery occurs beside reference to sexual immorality also in Matthew 15.19 and Hebrews 13.4. The word translated 'sexual immorality' is the Greek word *porneia*, which lies behind our English word pornography. Matthew's version of the divorce saying, which we will consider in the next chapter, includes *porneia* as a ground for allowing divorce and, as we shall see, people have proposed a range of possibilities based on the word's meaning, including sexual immorality, adultery and incestuous marriage. The *porn*- word group has its origins as a reference to prostitution, in particular, and this meaning is evident in the neutral description of Rahab in Hebrews 11.31 and James 2.25. It usually appears in the context of disapproval such as in the account of the prodigal son's exploits (Luke 15.30), and in Revelation's depiction of Rome as the unrepentant prostitute sitting on the seven hills (17.1–5, 15–16; 18.3, 9; 19.2; 14.8).

Matthew has Jesus declare that prostitutes along with tax collectors will make it into the kingdom of God before the chief priests and elders of the people (21.31–32). The probable presence of women among tax collectors at the meals where Jesus was sometimes present and which caused offence, may indicate that some were prostitutes who in such special meals elsewhere would often engage their trade. Herod Antipas' birthday feast aptly illustrates some of the typical sexual play (Mark 6.17–29). Possibly among those described as sinners in such accounts were prostitutes. The woman who anointed Jesus' head in Mark or his feet in Luke 7 may have been one, based on her equipment and Luke's mention of her sinful reputation, which his hearers would probably have understood in sexual terms; but we have no way of knowing for sure.

Paul tackles the issue of prostitution directly in 1 Corinthians 6.13–16. He begins by apparently citing slogans, which the Corinthians espouse and may even be quoting back to him. '"All things are lawful for me", but not all things are beneficial. "All things are lawful for me", but I will not be dominated by anything' (6.12). The danger of being dominated by something (or someone else) is fundamental to Paul's argument. He has just reminded the Corinthians of their conversion, which entailed leaving the old behind and coming under new lordship. Next he addresses a common argument which equates desire for food and desire for sex and makes both ethically neutral: '"Food is meant for the stomach and the stomach for food", and God will destroy both one and the other' (6.13).[37] Paul's response effectively declares that there is a higher authority to be taken into account, namely God. Alternatively, the slogan also includes the words, 'God will destroy both', implying that what we do about food and sex does not matter.[38]

Paul then declares the implication of the Christian's new relationship: 'The body is meant not for fornication but for the Lord, and the Lord for the body. And God raised the Lord and will also raise us by his power. Do you not know that your bodies are members of Christ?' (6.13–15). Paul assumes that Christians belong body and soul to God and the power and influence should lie here. It then becomes clear why he sees this as conflicting with engagement with a prostitute: 'Should I therefore take the members of Christ and make them members of a prostitute? Never! Do you not know that whoever *is united to* a prostitute becomes one body with her? For it is said, *"The two shall be one flesh."* But anyone *united* to the Lord becomes one spirit with him' (6.15–17). The issue is not just rival loyalties, but rival connections and influences. Thus Paul is returning to the issue of what should dominate. His assumption, based on a particular understanding of Genesis 2.24, which he quotes, is that through sexual intercourse one unites oneself to another human being in a way that actually puts one under their influence in some way. In this context the words which follow, 'Shun fornication!' must mean: 'Do not have sexual intercourse with prostitutes!' The rationale continues in the explanation which follows: 'Every sin that a person commits is outside the body; but the fornicator sins against the body itself' (6.18).[39]

His argument is that our bodies are affected when we engage with someone in sexual intercourse. That is the implication of his reading of Genesis 2.24, so that we effectively wrong ourselves because we come under someone else's influence. With a kind of serious playfulness Paul concludes, on the one hand, by using another description of the Christian's new state of being as a temple, a place of God's dwelling, and, on the other, by playing with the details of the commercial transaction with the prostitute, possibly also linked to a temple, though that is uncertain,[40] but in any case reversing the image. Who is buying whom? Christ has bought the Christian. The Christian should not be buying the prostitute. 'Or do you not know that your body is a temple of the Holy Spirit within you, which you have from God, and that you are not your own? For you were bought with a price; therefore glorify God in your body' (6.19–20).

The assumption in Paul's argument is that sexual intercourse actually does something of a permanent nature to people. It sets up a rival sphere of influence to that created by our having been joined to Christ. Paul's assumption coheres with the notion behind the use of Genesis 2.24 in Mark 10 according to which something permanent is created, namely indissoluble marriage. One might see Paul creating an inconsistency here, since if sex with a prostitute creates a rival body of influence, does not the same happen in legitimate marriage? Clearly Paul was able to hold both ideas together, though he never addresses it as an issue. He would doubtless have seen marriage 'in the Lord' as belonging within the body and not something competing with it. This is the assumption in what follows where he sees Christian marriage as providing the appropriate place for sexual passions and helping ensure there is no leakage through engagement in prostitution, including by would-be celibates who end up not coping with the ambitions of their spirituality. Prostitution as well as any joining with the world, as 2 Corinthians 6.14—7.1 indicates, whether in marriage or otherwise, would constitute the same kind of conflict, and it is not surprising that there we see the same cultic language and warning about contamination.

Like its Hebrew equivalent, *zěnûth* which has similar origins, the word *porneia* came to be used more broadly for a range of acts of sexual wrongdoing. These include incest, which features among the warnings of *Jubilees* and the *Damascus Document*. In the NT it rarely appears. Mark reports John the Baptist's objection to Herod Antipas marrying his half-brother's wife (6.17–18), a particularly strict application of Leviticus 18.16; 20.21, with which we must assume Jesus would have concurred. Some have argued that in the instructions to Gentiles by the apostles in Acts 15.20, 29; 21.25 the word *porneia* refers to the prohibition of incestuous marriages in Leviticus 18, and, as noted above, see it in Matthew's divorce sayings. Paul uses it of alleged incest in 1 Corinthians 5.1, of a man living with his father's wife, clearly not his own mother, so either a second wife (perhaps now widowed) or a concubine.

Mixed marriages

In much Jewish literature we find reference to the problem of inter-marriage with Gentiles as a key aspect of sexual immorality.[41] The strictest practice is found in Tobit, where marriage must be not only with another Jew, but within one's own extended family, commonly designated endogamy (1.9; 4.12–13; similarly Judith 8.1). Endogamy was common practice in the world of the NT with the exception of Rome, where exogamy was more common.[42] We see endogamy practised in Genesis among the patriarchs. There is some evidence that this was also important within the priestly tribe of Levi. Slightly less strict but severe in its implications is the prohibition of marriage with any Gentile, having its roots in demarcation from Gentiles and their idolatry and given particular emphasis in Ezra (9.1–2; 10.10–11) and Nehemiah (13.23–29), and, more narrowly, also Deuteronomy 7.3–4. *Jubilees* champions this approach, but primarily on grounds that the nations are sexually immoral. The strict line repeats itself through *Aramaic Levi Document*, Theodotus, 4QMMT, Pseudo-Philo, where Tamar declares it a much greater evil than incest (9.5), the *Testament of Job* and *2 Baruch*, sometimes even refusing marriage to proselytes (*Jubilees*, and probably the *Additions to Esther*). Levi and Phinehas were its heroes. Against this stands the book of Ruth, the surprising disinterest of the *Temple Scroll* and the *Damascus Document*, and notably *Joseph and Aseneth*, which exploits the loophole Joseph's marriage provided, to depict divine sanction for marriage to Gentiles who convert and even has Levi change sides (22.11–13).

One might expect the issues to have arisen as Jews and Christians mingled in the new Christian communities, but we find no trace. Unlike Ezra, who breaks up mixed marriages, Paul exhibits great flexibility, allowing divorce where the unbelieving partner wants it, but otherwise encouraging believers to remain with their unbelieving spouses. We may see a reflection of the issue in 2 Corinthians 6.14—7.1, where Paul employs language which in a Jewish context would have been applicable to the issue of mixed marriages: not being yoked with unbelievers, joining righteousness and lawlessness, light with darkness, Christ and Belial, the temple of God and idols. Paul may be addressing mixed marriages with unbelievers here, namely, that believers should not initiate such marriages, but most see the issues there as much broader, such as in the similarly abruptly intro- duced and unexpected comments about wrongdoing which Paul adds in 12.20–21, though it could include intermarriage.[43] The imagery of yoking unequal animals derives from Leviticus 19.19, which along with Deuteronomy 22.9–11 served to counter mixed marriages in some Jewish texts (e.g. 4QMMT). Paul's insistence that if widows remarry, they do so 'in the Lord' (1 Cor. 7.39) implies a stance against intermarriage, though it is not clear whether he reserves it for widows as especially susceptible to outside influence[44] or assumes it applies to all. Earlier he urged Corinthians to remain in mixed marriages (7.12–16), as 1 Peter 3.1–2 later also assumes, but initiating new ones was something different. Revelation 2.14 alludes to Balak and Balaam, and by implication to enticement to sexual intercourse with foreigners, though here and in 2.20–21 the allusion functions metaphorically to warn against false teachers.

Sexual wrongdoing

More often the word *porneia* appears in a general sense of sexual wrongdoing without further specification, such as in lists (Mark 7.21; Matt. 15.9; 1 Cor. 5.11; 6.9; 2 Cor. 12.21; Gal. 5.19–21; Eph. 5.3, 5; Col. 3.5; 1 Tim. 1.10; Rev. 21.8; 22.15) and in broader contexts of sexual immorality (John 8.41; 1 Cor. 6.18; 1 Thess. 4.3; Rev. 9.21) and the sexually immoral (1 Cor. 5.9–10; 10.8; Heb. 12.16). This may be its meaning in Acts 15.20, 29. It frequently occurs in association with notions of revelry and debauchery, and sometimes drunkenness (Rom. 13.13–14; 1 Cor. 5.11; 6.9–10; 1 Pet. 4.3; Gal. 5.19; Eph. 4.19).

In some instances we can go beyond general terms to discern the matrix in which authors understood sexual wrongdoing, or at least recognize issues with which they confront us. This is so in 1 Thessalonians 4.3–8, where Paul is expounding to the recipients of his letter how they should now live and doing so on the basis of instructions he had already passed on to them in the name of Christ (4.1–2). Paul employs words associated traditionally with the Temple cult, but which had been widened to apply to the state in which people should be in relating to God anywhere. We saw such language applied in Romans 1.24. Thus he speaks of their 'sanctification': 'For this is the will of God, your sanctification: that you abstain from fornication' (4.3), and, typically of the careful rhetorical composition of his day, he returns to this opening theme as he closes this section, when he writes: 'For God did not call us to impurity but in holiness' (4.7). What comes in between is another instance where translators have to become interpreters and so leave other options behind.

> that each one of you know how to control your own body [or: how to take a wife for himself] in holiness and honor, not with lustful passion, like the Gentiles who do not know God; that no one wrong or exploit a brother or sister [Greek: brother] in this matter.   (1 Thess. 4.4–6)

NRSV fortunately identifies two of the options in 4.4. The Greek *skeuos* could refer to the man's own body[45] or to his wife[46] or to his penis.[47] Interestingly we find a similar dilemma in one of the documents at Qumran, which reads: 'Moreover do not treat with dishonour the "vessel" (or "wife") of your [bo]som' (4QInstr[b]/4Q416

2 ii.21), but could refer to the penis in one's lap.[48] The context in my view favours 'wife' there, but we cannot be sure. The words which NRSV translates by 'take a wife', suggesting marriage, can also mean 'treat or control a wife'. The following words provide further relevant context, for Paul declares this is not to be 'with lustful passion', literally, 'in the passion of desire/lust', 'like the Gentiles who do not know God'. Paul associates Gentiles with driven passions also in Romans 1.24–27. Paul then continues the same single sentence which began in 4.3 in a way that provides us with further clues about the meaning: 'that no one wrong or exploit a brother in this matter'. NRSV adds 'or sister' but given the importance of gender issues in understanding ancient marriage practice it is better to stay with just, 'brother'.

We are therefore left wondering how all this fits together. How does a man through lustful treatment in handling his body (or his wife or his penis) lead to transgression or taking advantage of another man? It is hard to see how his treatment of his own wife or taking a wife would affect others, whereas the way he treats his own body (or penis) certainly could. The wronging of another man could be through sexual exploitation, involving the kind of same-sex behaviour deplored in Romans 1, also on the basis of such lustful passion. The Greek words used here for wronging and exploitation appear better to reflect the notion of wronging by taking advantage of.[49] This could be through seeking sexual favour from another man's household[50] or more specifically by adultery with another man's wife.[51]

Alternatively, the text uses the language for taking a wife, usually with sexual implications, and so addresses excessive lust, reflecting the disapproval of passions expressed by some moral philosophers, some of whom saw sexual intercourse as legitimate only for the purposes of begetting and not to be accompanied by passion. Thus Fredrickson sees Paul's espousal of passionless sex here and in 1 Corinthians 7.2,[52] but as we have seen, Ellis and Deming have challenged this and in any case in his article Fredrickson appears to focus less on denying passions altogether and more on the evils of excessive passion. He cites Pseudo-Phocylides, 'Do not deliver yourself wholly unto unbridled sensuality towards your wife, for "eros" is not a god, but a passion destructive of all' (193–4), and writes of 'over-indulgence in pleasures' and loss of honour through loss of control.[53] This still leaves the connection with 4.6 unclear. There Paul does not write of the sister (wife) being wronged but a brother. Another option is to see a change in subject altogether at 4.6 and to understand wronging and taking advantage of a brother as a warning against economic exploitation, and 'in this matter' as meaning 'in a business matter'.[54] Richard even argues that the words translated 'lustful passion' have nothing to do with sex, but already address greed.[55]

Sex and 'flesh'

As in Romans 1 and 1 Corinthians 7, the emphasis is more probably on sexual passion, referring to its excess and misdirection rather than to natural sexual responses, which Paul sees finding a place within marriage. 'Desires' are potentially dangerous. Paul regularly draws attention to this, though often in a way that the focus is broader than just sexual desires/lust. Thus in Romans 6.12 he warns against the reign of sin in one's body which makes people obey the body's desires, becoming their slaves, instead of having dominion over them (cf. 6.14). In Romans 7 he describes this state of affairs as where the command not to desire what is forbidden even activates all kinds of such desire and plunges people into spiritual and moral death. These are the desires of the flesh (13.14). In writing to the Galatians Paul tells them to walk in the Spirit and not gratify the desires of the flesh (5.16), just as later, to the Romans, he writes of two opposing ways of living: according to the flesh or according to the Spirit. People can easily hear this language as indicating that Paul is pitting the soul against the body and treating the body and all its desires as evil. Closer attention to detail shows that this is mistaken, as well as a misrepresentation of Paul's view of human beings. For he does not set the material and spiritual worlds as opposites in this way, but uses the contrast, flesh–spirit more subtly. We see this in his exposition in Galatians, where he identifies what he means by the works of the flesh:

> Now the works of the flesh are obvious: fornication, impurity, licentiousness, idolatry, sorcery, enmities, strife, jealousy, anger, quarrels, dissensions, factions, envy, drunkenness, carousing, and things like these. (Gal. 5.19–21)

These are clearly not about bodily functions and instincts, but about attitudes and behaviours. The 'flesh' is then about a way of being, opposed to God and God's ways. In the same passage he then describes the fruit of the Spirit: 'By contrast, the fruit of the Spirit is love, joy, peace, patience, kindness, generosity, faithfulness, gentleness, and self-control' and goes on to say that 'those who belong to Christ Jesus have crucified the flesh with its passions and desires' (5.24). This is not about physical suicide but about putting an end to a way of being. Elsewhere Paul can speak of his own desire to see people (1 Thess. 2.17) or the Lord (Phil. 1.23) and later writings sometimes remove any ambiguity by adding 'evil' or 'senseless' to the word 'desire' to make clear that there are good and evil desires (Col. 3.5; 1 Tim. 6.9). Concern with the danger of desires, possibly sexual, continues to be reflected in the letters to Timothy and Titus (1 Tim. 6.9; 2 Tim. 2.22; 3.6; Titus 2.12; 3.3), including the reference to the young widows who live for pleasure (1 Tim. 5.6). Paul nowhere singles out pleasure as problematic, unlike Philo, Josephus and the Stoics. References to the pleasure of life as choking growth in Luke 8.14 and to pleasure in Titus 3.3; James 4.1, 3; 2 Peter 2.13 appear not to have a sexual reference. The reference to 'evil talk' in Ephesians 4.29 may be sexual.

James uses 'desire' in a sexual sense metaphorically in association with the conception and birth of sin (1.14–15). 1 Peter can speak generally of the danger of desires (1.14), 'desires of the flesh' (2.11; similarly 4.3–4). 1 John challenges its hearers to see the lusts of the flesh as belonging to the passing age (2.15). Jude's attack on opponents employs the language of lusts (16, 18), having compared them with recalcitrant Israel in the wilderness, the angels who abandoned their heavenly places, and the people of Sodom, who committed sexual immorality by going after 'other flesh' (5–7). The latter may refer to their plan to rape the angels visiting Lot, or to their propensity for same-sex relations. 2 Peter also employs these images, adding Noah's generation, and describing them all as engaging their flesh in depraved lust (2.10), and depicting opponents as indulging their own lusts (2.18; 3.3) and as like dogs returning to their vomit and pigs to their squalor. This all appears to be the rhetoric of enflamed conflict rather than descriptions of actual practice.

5

Divorce and remarriage

Of all the matters pertaining to sexuality, divorce and remarriage receive the most attention in the NT. We have two versions of an anecdote in which Pharisees confront Jesus with the issue head-on (Mark 10.2–9; Matt. 19.3–9). There are five versions of a saying of Jesus on the theme, two of which are attached to the anecdote (Mark 10.11–12; Matt. 19.9); the single sayings in Matthew 5.31–32, Luke 16.18 and 1 Corinthians 7.10–11. Paul discusses the issue in 1 Corinthians 7.10–16 in particular in relation to mixed marriages. It appears also in Matthew's account of Mary and Joseph, where Joseph apparently assumes he must divorce Mary (1.18–19).

Mark 10.2–9 and the question about divorce

We begin with the story in Mark 10.2–9, which most hold to be the earlier version, and which Matthew revised in his expanded Gospel perhaps some 15 or so years later.[1] Not all see the sequence in this way, some arguing either that Mark has abridged Matthew or that Matthew independently draws on an equally early if not earlier version of the story which existed independently of Mark.[2] This is not the place to discuss these differences in detail, but we shall keep an eye on them for where they could influence the way we understand what is being said.

Mark introduces his account very concisely with the report that some Pharisees approached Jesus asking him, 'Is it lawful for a man to divorce his wife?' Mark adds that they were testing Jesus. Their question and Mark's account of it already raise a number of questions as we seek to understand what is going on. Why would this question function as a test? What would Jesus have to do to pass or fail the test? What made them want to test Jesus in particular on this issue? What kind of law were they talking about? Why do they speak only of a man divorcing, not a woman?

Divorce in context

Some of the answers emerge from the immediate context. The law is the biblical law which both parties as well as Mark believed was given by Moses. Thus Mark reports: 'He answered them, "What did Moses command you?" They said, "Moses allowed a man to write a certificate of dismissal and to divorce her"' (10.3–4). In fact the only reference to divorce in biblical law is incidental and occurs in Deuteronomy 24.1–4, where the focus is what happens when a man divorces his wife, who then remarries, is then divorced or widowed, and the original husband wants to remarry her. It declares such a remarriage 'abhorrent' because 'she has been defiled' in relation to him. The prohibition may be targeting husbands who hope to profit as a result of an accumulation of dowries,[3] but the focus is clearly on issues of defilement both of the woman and of the land. The Greek translation even speaks of both defilements, using the same word.[4] Only incidentally do we find reference to what is clearly assumed to be standard practice: a man could divorce his wife. Fortunately, it tells us more: the divorce was accompanied by a certificate, the *get*, a distinctive feature of Israel's law,[5] and there had to be some ground for the divorce, which is named as 'something shameful'. This may reflect development from a stance where divorce was uncontrolled practice, like the expulsion of Hagar at Sarah's whim (Gen. 16.3; 21.9–14), though itself not divorce, to an attempt to regulate divorce through the courts to protect people's (especially women's) rights.[6] The chief function of the certificate was to declare that the woman was free to marry someone else and could not be accused of committing adultery against her former husband if she did.

The incidental reference to the ground for divorce, 'something shameful', is vague. If it had referred to adultery by the wife, then according to Leviticus 20.10 and Deuteronomy 22.22 she and her adulterous male partner were to be put to death. Assuming those formulating Deuteronomy 24.1–4 were aware of this, they would hardly therefore have envisaged adultery here – the woman would be dead! This might change where capital punishment for adultery was no longer in force or could no longer be enforced because of new jurisdictions.[7] Then the possibilities for the meaning of these words could range from adultery to something much less. The Theodotion text of Susanna, for instance, assumes that 'something shameful' would include adultery (63). Similarly Philo appears to have interpreted it in this way (*Special Laws* 3.30–1). In addition, the more polygyny became less common,[8] the more divorce became the option and so the more important it became to be clear about what could justify divorce. The earlier stance is reflected in Pseudo-Philo's account of Samson's parents, where Manoah's response to Eluma's sterility was not that he divorce her, but that he take an additional wife (42.1–3).

A negative stance towards divorce appears in Malachi 2.14–16, where the Hebrew text reads: 'He hates divorce', but probably originally read: 'I hate divorce'. The context deplores people being unfaithful to the wife of their youth, and probably divorce on grounds of aversion (hate), but it is also employing this image to confront unfaithfulness in Judah's relation to God.[9] Davies and Allison see it as likely to have influenced Jesus' radical stance.[10] Its Greek translators clearly understood it this way.[11] Before the publication of the additional fragments of the *Damascus Document* found at Qumran, many saw its prohibition of having more than one wife during one's lifetime (4.21) as targeting divorce, but the fragments clearly show divorce and remarriage as accepted, so that its concern here is polygyny.[12]

Later rabbinic tradition preserved in the Mishnah (*m. Gittin* 9.10) and the Babylonian Talmud (*b. Gittin* 90a) reports debates between the Pharisaic houses of Hillel and Shammai during the first century BCE and after, over what were legitimate grounds for divorce, the school of Shammai favouring a narrow definition which included adultery and sexual immorality, the school of Hillel favouring a much broader definition which included being unpleasing or even burning the cakes![13] Given the likelihood that these accounts have some historical value, then it would not be surprising to find that the topic came up in Jesus' encounters with Pharisees.

The incidental reference in Deuteronomy 24.1–4 leaves a lot of unanswered questions. It is very likely that divorce sometimes took place without provision of a bill of divorce, especially among the poor, who would not have been able to read it anyway, just as marriages would have been established by many without written contracts. To divorce meant effectively sending one's wife (or one of one's wives) away, just as Abraham expelled Hagar at Sarah's request (Gen. 16.3; 21.9–14). Unless she was well off she then had to find an alternative household if she was to survive or resort to some other means of supporting herself, such as prostitution. Most often she would return to her father's household or move as quickly as possible to marry again, becoming a member of her new husband's household. This is what we should expect in a male-dominated society where survival depended on belonging to some man's household and there was no such thing as a welfare state.

While the dominant pattern was for men to divorce wives, there is also evidence that Jewish women could initiate divorce.[14] As Satlow puts it, 'In ancient Semitic law, and among Jews in the prerabbinic period, the right of divorce was bilateral: a husband or wife could initiate a divorce.'[15] We find evidence of this among the papyri found at Elephantinum already in the fifth century BCE[16] and in the early second-century CE Babatha archive of documents found in the Murabba'at caves of the Judaean desert.[17] In the Roman world both men and women initiated divorce.[18] Thus Satlow concludes: 'Some (most?) Jews in first-century Palestine may also have allowed a woman to initiate a divorce. Rabbinic law clearly changed this, giving the husband the unilateral right to divorce his wife.'[19] The Augustan laws (*Lex Iulia de adulteris* 18 BCE) designed to strengthen family law required divorce where adultery had taken place. This would have influenced the ways Jews interpreted their own laws, where it was also probable that they saw such texts as Deuteronomy 24.1–4 as implying that adultery required divorce, the woman having become unclean for her husband. This view is attested in *Jubilees* (33.9; also *Test. Reuben* 3.15), *Genesis Apocryphon* (20.15) and probably in the story of Joseph and Mary (Matt. 1.18–19). It is not always assumed as mandatory. Thus Ben Sira sees the need to commend divorcing a recalcitrant or adulterous wife (Sir. 25.26; similarly Prov. 18.22a LXX).

Jesus' response in Mark 10.2–9

Returning to the anecdote in Mark 10 we can see that the issue of divorce was most likely a hot topic at the time of Jesus. That some Pharisees want to 'test' Jesus on the issue may simply indicate that they want to know where he stands or perhaps that they already have a whiff of suspicion that he takes a controversial stance. In the initial exchange Jesus asks the Pharisees about what Moses had commanded. Jesus knows the answer so his question redirects theirs. Nothing suggests that by referring to Moses Jesus is thereby disqualifying what is said, as though Moses' commandments did not matter. The Pharisees reply with their distillation from the incidental reference to divorce in Deuteronomy 24.1–4, that it implied that Moses was instructing people to divorce and supply a certificate of divorce. Jesus then comments: 'Because of your hardness of heart he wrote this commandment for you' (Mark 10.5). Some take this to mean that Moses gave this commandment in order to harden their heart.[20] Most, however, read it as indicating that Moses gave the instruction because of people's hardness of heart. Instone-Brewer sees it as alluding to God's confrontation of Israel in Jeremiah 4.4 LXX.[21] Jesus does not rubbish what Moses said, but by implication declares that if the people were not so hard-hearted, they would not have needed such a provision.[22] By implication, people should be trying to live in a way that they do not have hard hearts, but instead do what God intended in the first place. Nothing in the context suggests an argument based on the beginning of a new order or the rejection of the old order and therefore a return to the original order.[23]

It is therefore at this point that he brings the two texts from the Genesis creation story which show how marriage was meant to be 'from the beginning' (10.6–8). This is a clever move, because Jesus avoids the trap of contradicting Moses and setting the law aside, yet also maintains his stricter position, which is that people should uphold what was God's original intention. It is also indicative of a shift of focus from the legal to the moral, as Harvey notes, and evokes creation in a way similar to what we find in Tobit 8.6–7.[24] As discussed above, the creation of human beings as consisting of two kinds, male and female (Gen. 1.27), is the basis for then interpreting Genesis 2.24 as their coming together as one flesh. Ben Sira can even describe divorce as cutting the wife off from the husband's flesh (25.26). In Hebrew the words for 'man' and 'woman' have such similar sounds that the focus in 2.23 on their being of the same substance, 'flesh of my flesh, bone of my bone' (used similarly of a permanent relationship in Genesis 29.14; Judges 9.2–3; 2 Samuel 5.1; 19.13, 14; 4QMMT B 39–49) is sustained and the two substances separated in woman's creation come together again as they join to become one flesh. The Greek translation also reports the making of woman from man, 'bone from my bone, and flesh from my flesh', but cannot reproduce the Hebrew play on words between man and woman, so that the focus falls slightly more on the numbers – two becoming one – than on common substances rejoining. The Greek translation, possibly already drawing on a different Hebrew text from ours, has the additional word 'two' in Genesis 2.24, so that it reads 'and the two become one flesh', reflected in the citation here in 10.8.[25]

Beyond these two biblical citations Jesus then declares: 'Therefore what God has joined together, let no one separate' (10.9). God's involvement may be seen in the act of their coming together – perhaps even in their being joined, if 'be joined' in Genesis 2.24 is understood as joined by God – or in the fact that God created things this way. The word 'joined' in the phrase 'what God has joined' is different from that found in Genesis 2.24. It can also mean 'yoked', as in two animals being yoked together for ploughing. This imagery for marriage occurs in 2 Corinthians 6.14 and in Sirach 25.8, where Ben Sira expresses concern that the pairing is compatible and not uneven (see also 26.7). Such imagery appears also in the Stoic Musonius Rufus' positive account of mutuality in marriage.[26] The word used for 'separate' is commonly used to describe divorce, so that in effect Jesus is saying: do not divorce those whom God has yoked together in marriage.

The argument that one should not undo what God has done speaks for itself and is typical of many of Jesus' pithy responses when confronted with controversy. They usually have two parts and make their point with effective simplicity. They include: 'the Sabbath was made for humankind, and not humankind for the sabbath' (Mark 2.27); 'There is nothing outside a person that by going in can defile, but the things that come out are what defile' (Mark 7.15); 'Those who are well have no need of a physician, but those who are sick' (Mark 2.17). It may well be that these alone were Jesus' original reply, and that people added the proofs from Scripture later, but one can only speculate.[27] The potency of Jesus' punchline in this instance is that to divorce is to undo what God has done and is therefore not to be tolerated. The Greek emphasizes the contrast by beginning the first part with the word 'God' and the second part with the word 'human being'. The extent to which this was a confronting statement designed to make people think, or a community rule, is not easy to determine.

It should not be seen as a setting aside of biblical law in an absolute sense.[28] Rather, it is typical of interpretations of the time which underline the law's seriousness by spelling out its implications, and so belongs within the framework of contemporary debate about the law's interpretation. It is significant that we find no report in the tradition according to which Pharisees or anyone else saw Jesus' stance here as overturning the law or setting Scripture aside.

Matthew 19.3–9

The second version of the anecdote is to be found in Matthew 19.3–9, where most assume that Matthew has revised Mark.[29] Matthew's account differs in some details from Mark's. It is basically the same in introducing Pharisees who are testing Jesus (19.3), and in including the allusion to Deuteronomy 24 (19.7–8), the citation of the Genesis texts (19.4–6a), and Jesus' punchline (19.6b). It differs in reversing the order of the allusions to Deuteronomy and Genesis; in including Jesus' statement about divorce and remarriage in the exchange (19.9), whereas Mark has Jesus make this statement only afterwards, privately, to his disciples (Mark 10.10–12); and in some minor subtle changes. Among these is the addition of the words 'for any cause' (19.3) to the Pharisees' question about divorce. This may appear to make no substantial difference, but it does prepare for Matthew's distinctive version of Jesus' saying, which actually does name a case and would be heard as alluding to Deuteronomy 24.1.[30]

Matthew differs from Mark in depicting Jesus as beginning his reply by citing the Genesis texts. He adds the confronting 'Have you not read', then, instead of Mark's 'But from the beginning' (which he brings later in 19.8), reads: 'The one who made them at the beginning' (19.4). In Matthew's version of Genesis 2.24, unlike in Mark's, its full text has manuscript support. It is only after Jesus declares, 'Therefore what God has joined together, let no one separate' (19.6b) that the reference to Deuteronomy 24 appears, and here the Pharisees introduce it: 'Why then did Moses command us to give a certificate of dismissal and to divorce her?' Jesus responds, as in Mark without disparagement of Moses: 'It was because you were so hard-hearted that Moses allowed you to divorce your wives, but from the beginning it was not so' (19.8). Some see significance in the different words in use here: they ask about what Moses *commanded*, and Jesus responds by referring to what Moses *allowed*, though in Mark we have the reverse where they refer to what Moses permitted and Jesus to what he commanded,[31] but the variations may simply reflect the fact that Moses could not command that people divorce their wives, whereas he could demand provision of a certificate.[32]

Of major significance is the saying which Matthew brings as the climax of the anecdote, which addresses both divorce and remarriage (19.9). Mark has a related saying, but given privately afterwards to the disciples (10.11–12). Matthew also has the feature of particular instruction to the disciples, but it has material without parallel in Mark, namely a saying about eunuchs to which we shall return below (19.10–12). Matthew's saying in 19.9, and Mark's in 10.11–12, belong to the five such sayings about divorce and remarriage found elsewhere in Matthew 5.31–32; Luke 16.18; and 1 Corinthians 7.10–11. They are all similar, yet each one has distinctive emphases.

The saying in Mark 10.11–12

We begin with those attached to the anecdotes. In Mark we read of a different location where apparently only the disciples are gathered, who 'asked him again about this matter' (10.10). It is interesting that Mark appends this story, since one could argue that the meaning of the anecdote is clear. On the other hand, we find this sequence quite frequently in Mark, where Jesus makes statements and then later the disciples seek and receive further instruction (e.g. 4.10–20; 7.17–23). This has less likely to do with Mark's need to find some place for additional material and more to do with ensuring instructions are clear for those communities of faith meeting in houses or equivalent needing to know how they should live in the world. Community concerns continue in the rest of Mark 10, in the instruction about children and about wealth. Thus Mark appears intent on conveying what Jesus meant to the people of his own day. It is highly likely that he knew of a saying of Jesus on the matter, as the parallels suggest, but now he shapes it to address the needs of those who will be listening to his gospel. Thus he has Jesus declare:

> Whoever divorces his wife and marries another commits adultery against her; and if she divorces her husband and marries another, she commits adultery. (10.11–12)

The subject matter is not just divorce on its own, but divorce and remarriage. Some have argued that the saying is not questioning divorce at all, but only remarriage.[33] Coming immediately after 10.9, which explicitly outlaws divorce, this would be surprising. The grounds for deeming remarriage 'adultery' lie in the assumption that the first marriage is still in existence. Others argue that the assumption is not in view and that 'adultery' is used metaphorically to describe divorce as an act against one's own marriage,[34] but this assumes the words operate at two levels, literal and metaphorical. Even if one might imagine divorce not followed by remarriage, this saying certainly does not recognize such a divorce in the first place.

There are two features unique to Mark's version of the saying not present elsewhere, at least among the Gospels. Mark writes of adultery being committed against a woman, the man's original wife.[35] This is 'a stunning reversal of convention'[36] and probably reflects that Mark writes in a context which laid greater emphasis on mutuality between husband and wife and less just on male ownership and adultery as theft.[37] This was certainly a trend in Roman understandings of marriage.[38] The second is that Mark has Jesus speak of a woman divorcing, reflected also in Paul. For many years people assumed that in Jewish law only men could divorce, but, as noted above, evidence now suggests that this was not exclusively so. Certainly both women and men could divorce in Roman law, and Mark's formulation may reflect also that influence.

The sayings in Matthew 19.9 and 5.31–32

When we turn to Matthew, we find that he has a saying about divorce and remarriage as part of Jesus' conversation with the Pharisees. It reads:

> And I say to you, whoever divorces his wife, except for unchastity, and marries another commits adultery. (Matt. 19.9)

As NRSV notes, some Greek manuscripts read: 'except on the ground of unchastity, causes her to commit adultery'; others add at the end of the verse 'and he who marries a divorced woman commits adultery'. In both instances we are probably dealing with influence from Matthew's other version of the saying.[39]

> It was also said, 'Whoever divorces his wife, let him give her a certificate of divorce.' But I say to you that anyone who divorces his wife, except on the ground of unchastity, causes her to commit adultery; and whoever marries a divorced woman commits adultery. (5.31–32)

There is some common ground with Mark in both sayings in that both declare remarriage adultery. This will be because both assume that the original marriage remains intact and by implication that divorce is never valid.[40] The claim in 5.32 that when a man divorces his wife he 'causes her to commit adultery' reflects the same assumptions, but in addition that she will be forced by circumstance to remarry, which was probably the most common option and so is treated here as generally the case.[41] The husband thus effectively forces the woman into adultery, thus rendering her unclean for him. Jesus' saying apparently wants to protect the woman from this.

Similarly when 5.32 speaks of committing adultery through marrying a divorced woman, it deems marriage permanent. The requirement matches what is demanded of priests according to Leviticus 21.7, that they not marry divorcees, as Isaksson noted, who also points to the presence of cultic language in contexts discussing marriage in Pauline writings (2 Cor. 6.14—7.1; Eph 2.18–22).[42] It is not clear however that Leviticus 21.7 plays a significant role, especially given the premise of indissolubility of marriage. Like Luke 16.18, Matthew 5.32, if referring to any divorced woman, could leave innocent divorcees with little hope. Some argue, indeed, that these texts extend the prohibition of remarrying expressed in Deuteronomy 24.1–4, so that it covers not only the original husband but everyone else.[43] In situations where divorce was legitimate, however, and so the first marriage legitimately dissolved, the charge of adultery could not hold. On the other hand, a woman divorced on grounds other than sexual wrongdoing, that is, illegitimately, would be in the worse position by far, since her original marriage is deemed still to be intact. Watson speculates that the original meaning of the anecdote about Jesus and the adulterous woman (John 7.53—8.11) relates not to an extramarital affair, but to a remarriage, and that the Pharisees are challenging Jesus' ruling that remarriage constitutes adultery. Jesus' call to the one without sin is directed to the original husband who divorced the woman in the first place.[44]

Neither saying in Matthew refers to a woman divorcing, unlike Mark, and neither names the person against whom the adultery is committed – clearly the original husband in both instances in 5.32, but possibly the original wife in 19.9, though she is not specified. Perhaps Matthew and similarly Luke, who both omit reference to the one against whom the adultery is committed, thought more in terms of adultery as an offence against God. Both sayings in Matthew are set over against Deuteronomy 24 ('Whoever divorces his wife, let him give her a certificate of divorce'). In 5.32 the saying belongs to the six contrasts between how the law is being heard and interpreted and how it should be. Coming immediately after the exposition of adultery in the second contrast (5.27–30), the reference to adultery here is doubly reinforced. Harvey argues that the focus here is not legal, as in Deuteronomy 24.1–4, but moral and belongs more in wisdom than legal tradition, though like the Mishnah in *m. Abot* 1.5 it uses legal language.[45] Perhaps, but people soon treated it as legal.

Of special interest is the qualifying phrase which occurs with slight variation in both sayings: 'except for unchastity' (19.9); and 'except on the ground of unchastity' (5.32). The word translated in both instances by 'unchastity' is *porneia*, which we met in the previous chapter. There is considerable debate about its meaning here. It could mean sexual immorality, such as adultery,[46] though the fact that the word for adultery is not used may indicate that the focus is wider,[47] or not adultery at all;[48] some even suggest prostitution, or that the author is simply using a different word on stylistic grounds to avoid repetition[49] but means the same thing. It is used beside the traditional word for adultery to mean the same thing in Jeremiah 3.8–9 LXX.[50]

It could refer to sexual immorality committed before the marriage, such as Deuteronomy 22.13–21 envisages, where the penalty, however, is stoning not divorce, though in the comparable situation where Joseph assumes this has happened to him he knows he must divorce.[51] This would significantly narrow the application and, as Davies and Allison note, make premarital sex worse than adultery.[52] It is difficult to see other indications which require this.

A third reading sees in *porneia* a reference to incestuous relations, that is, marriage forbidden according to the laws of Leviticus 18.[53] Some see this as of particular relevance for what follows the anecdote in Matthew 19.3–9, namely 19.10–12, which they see as directed to special cases in the Matthean church where Gentiles have joined the Church with incestuous marriages, who must divorce and then remain unmarried, like eunuchs.[54] A similar concern, it is argued, lies behind the so-called apostolic decree in Acts 15.29[55] and was a preoccupation in the sectarian literature of Qumran.[56] This interpretation needs to assume that in Matthew's church people would not follow the usual pattern of simply treating such marriages as invalid in the first

place and so not requiring divorce.[57] The word *porneia* does not
occur in discussions of incest in Leviticus 18 or in patristic literature,
whereas its immediate context in Matthew's use is clearly Deuteronomy
24.1–4.[58] This makes it improbable that *porneia* refers to incest here.

Before exploring the implications of Matthew's sayings in this regard,
we need to note another alternative interpretation, which disputes
that Matthew envisages any exceptions at all, and translates the sayings along the lines that it means 'not even in the event of *porneia*',[59]
though most see this as not the most natural reading of the Greek.

The advantage of seeing here a reference to adultery is that this
would cohere with the widespread understanding that divorce is not
only an option, but also a necessity where adultery has taken place,[60]
as noted above under 'Divorce in Context'. If Matthew has Jesus
prohibit divorce except where adultery has taken place, it raises the
question of whether Jesus' stance is really the position later attributed
to the School of Shammai in interpreting Deuteronomy. Supporting
this is the citation of Deuteronomy 24 in Matthew 5.31 and the
formulation of the exception in words which, translated literally, read
'except for the matter of sexual immorality', which recalls 'shameful
matter', using the same (legal) word for matter found in Deuteronomy
24.1.[61] Thus Instone-Brewer sees Jesus in Matthew upholding Moses'
teaching in Deuteronomy 24.1–4 and interpreting it strictly.[62] The
difficulty facing this view is that in the anecdote Matthew shows Jesus
as setting his teaching in some sense in contrast to Deuteronomy 24,
when he introduces it with the word 'but' in both 19.8b and 19.9, which
here serves to contrast Jesus' teaching with what Moses allowed,
corresponding to the contrast in 5.31–32.[63]

There is a larger question beyond Matthew's two sayings. Was
Matthew toning down Jesus' absolute prohibition of divorce,[64] perhaps
wanting to show Jesus as standing in closer conformity with Moses'
teaching? The contrast just noted makes that unlikely. Or was he
making explicit what was arguably already implicit in the sayings in
Mark and elsewhere? Instone-Brewer claims this is so.[65] But not many
will go with him beyond that to assume that this should also include
seeing a range of other things as valid grounds for divorce, such as
those listed in Exodus 21.10–11 (provision of food, clothing and
sexual love).[66] Matthew is very specific in naming what was the exception, and we may assume that both his hearers and those of Mark, Paul
and Luke, along with good Roman citizens, would have agreed.

The saying in Luke 16.18

Luke brings his saying in a similar context to Matthew and it serves a similar end. Thus just as in Matthew Jesus' teaching on divorce belongs to the proof that Jesus takes the law seriously and spells out what it really means, so Luke uses the saying to make the point that with the coming of Jesus a broader battlefront has emerged where not only the law and the prophets and John the Baptist, but also the kingdom of God is under assault (16.16). The context confronts monetary greed (16.1–8, 9–13, 14–15). Moses and the prophets and now Jesus testify against it, as the rich man who neglected Lazarus is to learn (16.19–31). In asserting, like Matthew, that not a jot or stroke of the law is to be discarded (16.17), Luke cites just one single illustration: Jesus' saying about divorce.

> Anyone who divorces his wife and marries another commits adultery, and whoever marries a woman divorced from her husband commits adultery. (16.18)

In its immediate context Luke may understand it as targeting above all men who divorce and remarry out of greed for more wealth through acquiring bigger dowries.[67] This strategy could, however, easily backfire as both Ben Sira (25.21 Hebrew version) and Pseudo-Phocylides (199–200) warn, since marrying a woman with a rich dowry could mean substantial loss on divorce. When the latter goes on to warn against multiplying marriages (205–6), it probably refers to such divorce and remarriage. Luke's saying probably derives from the common sayings source he shares with Matthew, usually designated as Q, though Matthew's and Luke's versions differ markedly. The matter is complicated by the fact that while, as most assume, Luke has used Mark, unlike Matthew he has not two versions of the saying but only one, which leads, in turn, to the suspicion that he has homogenized the two. Perhaps, then, Matthew's in 5.32 is closer to what was originally in Q and Luke has modified it in the light of Mark 10.11–12.[68]

Turning to the saying, itself, it reflects the common assumption that the original marriage still exists and cannot be dissolved by divorce, so that any remarriage must therefore constitute adultery. Of the two instances cited, the first, as in Mark, assumes an offence against the former wife, though, like Matthew, Luke does not specify this. The second envisages adultery against the woman's former husband on similar grounds. It could be translated as saying that the woman has not been divorced by her husband, but has divorced herself from her husband,[69] in which case, it may preserve an echo of Mark's statement about a woman doing the divorcing. On either count, adultery is being committed against her original husband, because the marriage remains intact and the divorce invalid.

The saying in 1 Corinthians 7.10–11

The final instance to consider is our earliest attestation, some 15–20 years before Mark, namely Paul's version of the saying in 1 Corinthians 7.10. Paul has just warned against having sex with prostitutes (6.12–20) and fielded a claim that it is better not to touch a woman (7.1). He does so in a way that both reflects his sympathy as one who has chosen celibacy and his awareness that marriage has a place in God's creation; helps keep sexual immorality at bay; is, like celibacy, God's gift; and is the proper place for married partners to meet each other's sexual needs (7.1–9). In 7.10 he directly addresses the married:

> To the married I give this command – not I but the Lord – that the wife should not separate from her husband (but if she does separate, let her remain unmarried or else be reconciled to her husband), and that the husband should not divorce his wife.

Paul is particularly sensitive in 1 Corinthians 7 to what is his own argument and advice and what claims higher authority. In citing 'the Lord' here, he will be drawing on what has been passed on to him as a saying of Jesus, which he has probably freely formulated. This includes that he first addresses wives, possibly reflecting actual situations at Corinth where women may have been promoting celibacy. The words 'not separate' reflect the language of divorce, as in Mark 10.9. 'Separate' is used in 7.10 of the wife and 'divorce' in 7.11 of the husband, which some suggest reflects the norm that the man divorces,[70] but both words are used of both interchangeably in what follows (7.12–13, 15).[71] In neither instance do we find any reason given, such as in the gospel sayings which declare remarriage adultery.

The words that NRSV encloses in brackets, 'but if she does separate, let her remain unmarried or else be reconciled to her husband' appear to be a bit of realism on Paul's part,[72] perhaps in the light of knowing that such divorces have already taken place in the community,[73] or were about to,[74] perhaps also reflecting Jesus' view on remarriage.[75] If these were people bent on celibacy, as Wire and others suggest,[76] it is hard to see why Paul would need to insist that they not remarry. The grounds for urging that the woman not remarry have probably less to do with his preference for celibacy, to which he does make exceptions, and more to do with an implicit acceptance of what is made explicit elsewhere, namely that to do so would be to commit adultery because the original marriage cannot be dissolved,[77] though this is not made explicit. In other words it appears to reflect an assumption that such divorces are not valid in the first place. This is the strength of Collins's observation that Paul probably did not see remaining unmarried and reconciling with their husbands as alternatives.[78]

Paul's realism finds expression also in what follows where he applies the saying to situations which its hearers would probably not have foreseen, namely, what to do about marriages where one partner has converted to Christian faith and the other has not. His sensitivity about authority continues as he quite self-consciously states that he is now giving his own advice, though Wire sees this as simply a rhetorical ploy to disarm his listeners.[79] He could simply have said that no marriage is dissoluble and people should live with the fact. He might have cited Genesis to show that these people, too, had become one flesh. Paul's advice leans in that direction. So it should apply where a man is happy to live with his unbelieving wife (7.12), and vice versa (7.13). At this point Paul employs the Jewish purity argument that one partner sanctifies the other and their children (7.14). Paul then faces the possibility that an unbelieving partner may want divorce. Then the believing spouse should not stand in the way and is not 'bound' (7.15), reflecting the language of the divorce certificate.[80] Insisting that they must stay together, when the unbelieving partner wants out, could become intolerable, so Paul declares: 'It is to peace that God has called you' (7.15). It made no sense to apply the divorce saying as an absolute rule, for Paul's faith rested on values which could override such rules. Paul would no more see himself in conflict with Jesus here than he does when he deliberately chooses not to follow Jesus' instruction that missionaries depend for their sustenance on local support and not work (9.14), though many criticized him for it (9.1–18). His realism is informed by a theology which transcends particular instructions in the light of principles of compassion at the core of his gospel, but that still does not undermine the norm which he finally reasserts in 7.16 with an additional argument: the prospect of converting one's spouse.

Mary and Joseph, Herod and John

The only other text of some relevance to the theme is one already visited in the course of discussion, namely the story of Joseph and Mary. The narrative appears to assume that Joseph had no choice but to divorce.[81] In his day capital punishment was not an option. Between public exposure and private dissolution of the relationship he chose the latter, and Matthew declares him righteous for choosing the more compassionate stance.

The issue of divorce may well have surfaced in discussions of John the Baptist, and presumably also Jesus, about the controversial divorce by Herod Antipas of his first wife (daughter of king Aretas), which was to have such fateful consequences for him; but Mark preserves only the concern about incest (6.17–18)[82] – which had fateful consequences for John!

Conclusions and unanswered questions

Engaging the NT sayings on divorce entails entering their world, where the options were more limited and the assumptions strange to modern ears. Such strangeness includes that adultery required divorce, that reconciliation was out of the question, that only adultery counted as grounds for divorce, and that sexual intercourse appeared to create a permanent state of affairs. There are a number of floating possibilities about which we may speculate. Would the perspective on adultery that saw it not just as an act but also as an attitude have played a role in determining the appropriateness or otherwise of divorce? There is no evidence that this connection was made or applied. Would the notion of reconciliation of estranged Israel, and especially of estranged humanity in Christ, have transferred in people's minds to reconciliation and forgiveness between marriage partners who for reasons of adultery, adulterous attitude or anything else have become estranged? We have no evidence that this was so.

It is noteworthy that the focus of concern in statements prohibiting divorce and remarriage is on keeping the commandment of not committing adultery. Only Mark makes it explicit that it is action against one's wife. To what extent do the other allusions to adultery seek to motivate the prohibition by appealing to the wrong done to the former marriage partner? Some have sought to explain the strictness of the divorce prohibition on the grounds that it often threw women into poverty and sometimes into prostitution. To what extent is this the silent agenda? This is certainly possible, although nowhere among the arguments does it appear. The situation of divorced women in the NT world was, indeed, serious. They could face serious discrimination, as in Sirach 7.26, which advises that a 'hated' woman, probably meaning a divorcee, is to be treated always with suspicion. Their best hope – and Matthew assumes their inevitable solution – was to remarry, unless of independent means, but that now seemed blocked by the declaration that to do so would be to commit adultery.

Individual trauma is not in focus. The concern is with divinely established order and on not transgressing it, in that sense operating primarily within a purity rather than an ethical framework, not to speak of a pastoral one; this is despite the fact that Matthew's first saying occurs within the context of the Sermon on the Mount. Even there, where compassion comes to the fore in the wider context of the contrasts, it is applied within an already established frame of reference about what is and is not divine order, rather than with particular concern for the plight of individuals beyond that. In this sense Luz and Fitzmyer rightly caution that we should not, in the interests of our preferred perspectives, make statements kind which in their original settings are harsh and uncompromising.[83]

We are also left wondering about what happened in situations where, as Matthew's sayings imply and others probably assume, adultery makes divorce mandatory. When Paul urges that women who have already divorced not remarry, but remain unmarried or return to their husbands, he is talking about those who voluntarily divorced, who could then voluntarily seek reconciliation. Presumably a spouse whose marriage has broken up because of his or her partner's adultery would be free to remarry.[84] What, then, of the so-called guilty party or the repentant guilty party, who is still barred from returning to the original marriage? Jewish divorce certificates declared a person no longer bound, language echoed in Paul's statement in 7.15; they were free to remarry. Some interpret Matthew 19.10–12 as implying those legitimately divorced should never remarry, but this is unlikely.[85] Only once do we hear of children in relation to marriage or divorce, namely in Paul's assurance that they are sanctified through the believing partner (1 Cor. 7.14). Apart from that we hear nothing of the impact of divorce or otherwise on children and families. We would dearly love to have Paul's hand to lead us through this maze of questions, but at most we can observe the flexibility he applied once and assume that gospel perspectives would dictate his answers.

He might also tell us how lasting he sees the effects of sexual intercourse with a prostitute and what happened when someone who had previously consorted with many prostitutes – there must have been many such men – converted to Christian faith. Are they considered to be of one flesh with one or many women or with none and what should they now do? If becoming one flesh does not stick so permanently in these instances, in what sense can it still be seen as sticking permanently in marriages? How watertight was the argument from the Genesis texts? What happened at the level of reality? A similar question arises in the ideal of marriage in Tobit, which sees marital partners determined by heaven (6.18; 7.11),[86] and by implication marriage without any prospect of divorce.

Thus despite the relative strength of evidence about divorce and remarriage in the NT, and its consistency in depicting marriage as indissoluble (except where broken by adultery), we are left with many historical questions about how these prohibitions worked themselves out, not to speak of the way they were understood and applied in diverse situations.

6

Has sex a future? The question of celibacy

According to Mark's Jesus, the answer to 'Has sex a future?' appears to be: no. In the age to come sexual relations will cease to be. 'When they rise from the dead, they neither marry nor are given in marriage, but are like angels in heaven' (12.25).

No sex in the age to come

Recently J. Harold Ellens has suggested the opposite: 'Jesus' implication was that she would be the partner of all seven brothers. Obviously Jesus was clear on the fact that heaven is a setting of holy promiscuity, where we shall enjoy total union with everyone who really delights us.'[1] The saying would then be about dispensing with weddings and marriage.[2] No one will own her as men were understood to own wives.[3] While there are some very positive values implicit in this suggestion, it seems unlikely to be the intention here. Being like the angels is unlikely to mean such 'holy promiscuity'. Luke's version goes in the opposite direction: angels live forever, so have no need to procreate; therefore to be like them is also not to need to engage in sex (Luke 20.35–36). He sees angels as celibate, and that was widely assumed. Mark's version does not say that explicitly, but both the context in Mark and the religious context make it unlikely that Jesus espouses here a future of open sex. It would imply setting biblical law aside in a way that would be unprecedented and be seen as outrageous. No such outrage is reflected in what follows in Mark.

In Mark's story Jesus is responding to a question from Sadducees who are trying to expose the absurdity of belief in resurrection (12.18–27). According to Acts 23.8 they reject this belief along with belief in angels (probably meaning angelic forms of resurrected life; cf. Dan. 12.2–3).[4] They present Jesus with a scenario in which a woman had seven successive husbands, from each of which she was widowed (12.20–22). They preface their account with reference to the provision for Levirate marriage in Deuteronomy 25.5–10, according to which, as they summarize it, 'Moses wrote for us that if a man's brother dies, leaving a wife but no child, the man shall marry the widow and raise up children for his brother' (12.19). We discussed the practice and this example above in dealing with polygyny. One can almost hear the snigger in their voices as they attempt to roll Jesus with their knock-down illustration and chuckle in male humour at its implications: 'In the resurrection whose wife will she be? For the seven had married her' (12.23). She will be having sex with seven brothers! The prohibition of the wife returning to her first husband in Deuteronomy 24.1–4 may also be in the background. It would be an abomination! Jesus does not try to assert that it would not be.

Jesus' reply, which does not dispute the Levirate provisions, consists of different kinds of arguments. First he declares: 'Is not this the reason you are wrong, that you know neither the scriptures nor the power of God?' (12.24). This has the effect of introducing what follows. The argument from Scripture comes in 12.26, where Jesus asks them: 'And as for the dead being raised, have you not read in the book of Moses, in the story about the bush, how God said to him, "I am the God of Abraham, the God of Isaac, and the God of Jacob"?' But first Jesus makes the statement in 12.25 about there being no marriage in the resurrection state, which in the context reflects an understanding of what the power of God can achieve (12.24). Referring to angels in his reply to the Sadducees may be astutely provocative. Jesus' response concludes with the neat, two-part, summary: 'He is God not of the dead, but of the living', adding, 'You are quite wrong' (12.27).

As noted in the discussion of 'Jesus' response in Mark 10.2–9' in the previous chapter (p. 85), such clever two-part one-liners may well have been typical of Jesus' replies and perhaps in many instances his only reply. This is possible here though not provable. It would mean that the rest of the reply might not have come from Jesus, but that need not mean that the views expressed would not have been consistent with Jesus' own views. They are now firmly embedded in the Jesus tradition. The bottom line here is that Jesus is responding to their attack by pulling the rug out from under their feet: in the resurrection age there will be no sexual relations.[5]

The statement, 'For when they rise from the dead, they neither marry nor are given in marriage, but are like angels in heaven' (12.25), appears in Matthew's version of the anecdote in identical form, except for minor differences in the opening words (22.30). Luke also brings the saying, but his version is more extensive:

> Jesus said to them, 'Those who belong to this age marry and are given in marriage; but those who are considered worthy of a place in that age and in the resurrection from the dead neither marry nor are given in marriage. Indeed they cannot die anymore, because they are like angels and are children of God, being children of the resurrection.
>
> (20.34–36)

Luke has greatly expanded the introduction, by including the basis for the contrast, namely that in this age people do marry, and by adding the words about those who will be worthy of a place in the age to come. This makes it clear that the statement to follow pertains only to those who will be resurrected, not to others, who face a different future fate. Most significant among Luke's revisions is the explanation why there is to be no sex in the age to come: the resurrected will no longer be mortal but will live forever like the angels. The implication is clear. If no one dies, then no one needs to be born. If no one needs to be born, then no one needs to have sex. The underlying assumption which Luke's revision shares with many in his world is that the only purpose of sexual intercourse is begetting children (e.g. 4 Macc. 16.9; 18.9; *Test. Issachar* 2.3; Philo, *Special Laws* 3.112).[6] Angels are immortal, therefore have no need to have sex. Some of the first hearers of Luke's Gospel may well have known the account of the angels who did have sex with women and begat giants, as recounted in Genesis 6 and in greater detail in *1 Enoch* 6—16.[7] In the latter account God has Enoch confront these angels by drawing to their attention that their behaviour was so inappropriate because they are immortal beings who do not die and therefore 'have no need of women' (15.6–7).

Luke could be simply spelling out what is implicit in Mark 12.25. That was probably his intention. Did Mark and Matthew see it this way? Finding an answer entails surveying a wide range of potentially relevant material both within and beyond the NT. Beginning within the Gospels themselves, both Mark and Matthew portray Jesus' response to the Pharisees' question about divorce as affirming marriage, including sexual union, and without particular reference to begetting children, matching the focus on reflecting the affirmation of sexual intimacy and companionship already implicit in Genesis 2, which he cites. This makes it less likely that they espouse Luke's view. It is surely significant that Luke even omits that episode altogether. As we shall see, he has a tendency also elsewhere to favour celibacy.

Strictly speaking, the angels, at least the Watchers, must have been able to respond to sexual stimuli, including those who chose not to, but the assumption behind the statement about the resurrection here in Mark 12.25 is likely to be that angels were asexual, that is, male in gender, but without sexual desire. Those to become like them in the resurrection would include women as well as men, but the power of God would enable both women and men to leave sexual desire behind. An essential element in early resurrection belief was that it was not revivification, but being raised to a transformed state of existence (Dan. 12.2–3; 1 Cor. 15.35–49). Alternatively, they were to live in a constant and successful state of suppressing their sexuality, but this is less likely. The potential impact of belief in a sexless resurrection state is enormous. As Streete observes, 'The eschatological perspective of the followers of Jesus and early Christianity, in which men and women "neither marry nor are given in marriage, but are like the angels in heaven" in the life of the "age to come" (Mark 12.25; Matt. 22.30; Luke 20.34–35), calls earthly marital and familial arrangements, including sexual behavior and reproduction into question (Matt. 10.26–27; Luke 14.26).'[8] Osiek and Balch draw attention to Cyprian's later appeal to this text in affirming consecrated virgins: 'That which we shall be, you have already begun to be'.[9]

Celibacy, sacred space and time

If the rationale for the saying in Mark 12.25 (Matt. 22.30) about there being no sexual relations in the age of resurrection is not that of Luke, we are left wondering why Jesus, or those depicting Jesus, saw the future this way. It stands in contrast, for instance, to the way many Jews saw future hope, including the authors of many of the documents found at Qumran. There the age of resurrection is one of abundance, including the abundance of progeny, even when they could speak of people living for a thousand years or more (1QS/1Q28 4.6b–8; CD 2.11b–12a; 7.6; 4QpPs^a/4Q171 1–10 iii.1–2a, 10–11),[10] similarly *1 Enoch* 10.17–18; *Sibylline Oracles* 3.594, 767–95; *Test. Abraham* 10.3. One document even cites the presence of the holy angels as the guarantee of human fertility (11Q14 1 ii.11, 14b). It has been customary to view the sectarian community reflected in some of the key documents from the caves as part of the Essene movement, which may well be. But that has often led to conclusions about these Qumran-related Essenes based on what Philo (*Every Good Man is Free* 75–91; *Contemplative Life* 1–2, 11–40, 63–90), Josephus (*Jewish War* 2.119–61) and Pliny (*Natural History* 5.17.4 (73)) report about the Essenes, namely that they were celibate and rejected sexual intercourse altogether. Josephus is an exception because he notes that there are some Essenes who do marry (*Jewish War* 2.160–1), but they engaged in sexual relations only for the purpose of begetting children and not otherwise. Josephus may be saving his own reputation here as one who had been an Essene and who married and so making this up, as Mason suggests.[11] He may well have known of Essenes who married, but then explained this in a way to appeal to what most moral philosophers of his day were espousing and which Luke also reflects, namely that the Essenes who did marry upheld the ideal of engaging in sex only for reproduction.

The detour via the Essenes and writings found at Qumran gives us a broader picture in which to understand at least one form of celibacy. For there were some who, according to the *Damascus Document*, were unmarried, just as there were others who married and 'lived in camps' (6.14—7.9a). Both are people of holiness and bound to live by the highest standards of holiness. Nevertheless the allusion to where they lived is a likely clue that those not living in camps were living somewhere where celibacy was particularly appropriate. Many have speculated that that place may have been at the site of Qumran, itself. This distinction between sacred space and secular space, to use a modern distinction which can misleadingly suggest that one is with God and one is without God, lies at the basis of Israel's faith. Thus the holy space of the Temple is set apart within the holy land. That distinction governs much of the legislation about purity and impurity and especially rites of purification to enable people and especially priests to enter holy space. Such views of holy space are also reflected in the instruction to the people that they refrain from sex before approaching Sinai (Exod. 19.15) and in David's allusion to the abstinence of his men before eating holy bread (1 Sam. 21.1–6). The people associated with Qumran similarly operated with these distinctions, even though they found themselves alienated from the Temple. Their hopes included a repossessing of the land and the holy city and a new or renewed Temple.

The distinction between sacred and non-sacred or less sacred space has major significance for understanding attitudes towards sexuality. Men's ejaculations rendered them in a state of impurity, from which they would need to undergo purification and they would not become clean until sundown. They were no more sin than were women's menstrual flows, for which there were also provisions for purification. It was above all important that no one enter sacred space in a state of impurity. The people of the *Damascus Document* and the *Temple Scroll* took this so seriously that they effectively banned sexual intercourse even in the holy city, which they saw as an extension of the Temple (11QT^a/11Q19 45.11–12; CD 12.1b–2a). Most did not go that far, but all agreed that no action producing impurity should occur in the Temple. That obviously meant: no sex in the Temple. This was not based on a low view of sex, but on the understanding that there are places where it belongs and places where it does not. Thus when people envisaged the age to come as life in the holy land with the holy city and its Temple, they envisaged a place for normal sexual life and a place where sex was inappropriate, as it had always been.

In the documents at Qumran we see signs of what this meant for them when they sought to construct their own sacred space in the interim until they regained the Temple. They insist therefore that people not come to their sacred gatherings in a state of impurity, including sexual impurity. Sometimes they reinforce this by referring to the presence of the holy angels (1QSa/1Q28a 1.25—2.9; 4QFlor/ 4Q174 1–2 3–4). Holy angels in holy space (including the war camp: 1QM/1Q33 7.5b–6) reinforce these requirements, just as holy angels in less sacred space will guarantee fertility and abundance. It all depended on the place. For *Jubilees* and the *Damascus Document* it also depended on the time. Unlike most other Jews then and since, their authors insisted that sexual intercourse should also not take place in sacred time, namely on the Sabbath (*Jub.* 50.8; CD 11.5; possibly 12.4; 4QHalakhah A/4Q251; cf. *b. Ketub.* 62b). None of this reflects a negative stance toward sexuality. Indeed, *Jubilees* highlights sexual union as a core element in the creation story and its fulfilment (3.1–7). But *Jubilees* also helps us see how sacred time and sacred space work. It deems the garden of Eden the most sacred space on earth (3.12; 4.26; 8.19) and accordingly has the first couple engage in sexual union outside the garden (3.5), before they enter it, and then refrain from intercourse while they are there, returning to have sex only after they leave the garden (3.34).[12] This account incidentally illustrates an understanding of sexual intercourse as celebrating union and intimacy and not as needing to be justified by the attempt to bear children. We should also note that with some exceptions celibacy was temporary – as long as one was in sacred space or, for some, in sacred time. This opened the possibility that some might remain for longer periods or even permanently in sacred space, such as those choosing not to live in camps according to the *Damascus Document*.

This understanding of space and time and the role of sexual relations within them has potential relevance for our understanding of what might have been meant by Mark 12.25, although in other respects they seem at odds. For most Jews, as it seems, embraced a future where land and Temple remained, including, therefore, a place where sexual relations had their place and a place where they were inappropriate. Accordingly they looked to a future which would be characterized by abundance, including abundant offspring. There may, however, be some points of connection between what we find in Mark 12.25 and what other Jews believed. Thus circles which insisted on abstinence from sex not only in sacred places, but also on the Sabbath, might envisage future hope as a permanent sacred space or Sabbath (cf. Heb. 4.9) and conclude that the eternal Sabbath will have no place for sex. Alternatively, where future space is envisaged as consisting entirely of sacred space or as a return to the paradise of Eden understood as a temple, then similarly sexual abstinence would be assumed. It remains speculative whether such perspectives influenced the thought behind Mark 12.25, but it is plausible.

144,000 virgins

The closest we come to this kind of thought in the NT is in the Book of Revelation, which depicts a future in which there will be no Temple. The holy city descends from heaven and the seer explains: 'I saw no temple in the city, for its temple is the Lord God the Almighty and the Lamb' (21.22). He then continues in language usually applied to the Temple: 'But nothing unclean will enter it, nor anyone who practices abomination or falsehood, but only those who are written in the Lamb's book of life' (21.27) and 'Nothing accursed will be found there any more' (22.3). The seer envisages future space as consisting entirely of holy space, a temple in itself, and uses imagery of the garden of Eden to depict its river and fruiting trees (see also Ezek. 47.1–12). Earlier in the work we find abundant references to the heavenly world as like a temple, a place of the constant celebration of worship (e.g. 4.1—5.14).

One of its visions of the future pertains directly to sexuality. It depicts 144,000 people standing beside the Lamb on Mount Zion (14.1). These 144,000 had featured already in 7.1–8, where they are depicted as coming from the twelve tribes of the people of Israel. They are then joined by myriads of others from every land and nation (7.9–10). The seer describes the 144,000 as those 'who have not defiled themselves with women, for they are virgins; these follow the Lamb wherever he goes. They have been redeemed from humankind as first fruits for God and the Lamb' (14.4). Thus they are male virgins. Given what is said in 7.1–10 these are a specific group identified within the larger number of the saved. There they are depicted as people of Israel compared with the others, who may be seen as Gentiles. We are dealing with numerical symbolism here, 12 times 12,000, rather than accurate predictions of numbers from each tribe, several of which were no longer in existence. The image of Israel may also be symbolic, that is, not a reference to Jews as opposed to Gentiles, which would also imply that the myriads of others need not be understood as only Gentile.

The explanation in 14.4–5 leads us beyond these distinctions by identifying the 144,000 as 'first fruits', but above all by describing them as those 'who have not defiled themselves with women, for they are virgins'. One might hear an echo of the Watcher myth about the angels who did defile themselves with women, and the explanation might mean no more than that the 144,000 are (like) good angels.[13] The difficulty then would be that the others would be the equivalent of the Watchers who did defile themselves and one wonders then why they are being given a place in the holy city at all. The emphasis on their being 'virgins' suggests that we have here an allusion to people who remained celibate. Understood within the framework of thought about the place of resurrection in Revelation as sacred space, these would then be those who had lived already during their life on earth as they will in the age to come. This would make sense of their being designated 'first fruits', the first to live like this. This sets them apart from the rest, although these are not disparaged for having engaged in sexual relations, for they, too, are now to join the 144,000 in this celibate bliss. The language of defilement belongs to the discourse of purity, related to the Temple (Deut. 23.10–11; Lev. 15.1–12, 16–18),[14] rather than to morality and so does not by implication disparage the others. Its formulation, however, reflects what for us is the alien world of such discourse, not least in its seeing women as particularly problematic.

It is possible therefore that the discourse of sacred space and time has at least influenced the understanding of the world to come in Revelation. Our discussion there has drawn attention to what appears to be a distinction in the mind of the author between two kinds of believers – those who are celibate, living now as they will then, and those who marry – but not in a way that disparages either. We do, in fact, find this twofold phenomenon attested in other NT writings and to these we turn.

Eunuchs for the sake of the kingdom

In Matthew's account of Jesus' controversy with the Pharisees over divorce, we find that after Jesus has stated, 'And I say to you, whoever divorces his wife, except for unchastity, and marries another commits adultery' (19.9), the disciples make the comment: 'If such is the case of a man with his wife, it is better not to marry' (19.10). The Greek word translated here as 'case' had already appeared in Matthew's version of the Pharisees' question about what 'case' warrants divorce (19.3). Here the meaning seems broader and the equivalent of 'situation'. The simplest explanation is to see the disciples saying that the dangers are so great in getting married, especially if when things do not turn out well and one contemplates divorce that option is blocked, that it is best to remain single. This then prompts the following response from Jesus:

> Not everyone can accept this teaching, but only those to whom it is given. For there are eunuchs who have been so from birth, and there are eunuchs who have been made eunuchs by others, and there are eunuchs who have made themselves eunuchs for the sake of the kingdom of heaven. Let anyone accept this who can. (19.11–12)

It is striking that a teaching of Jesus is made optional, a notion doubly reinforced on either side of the teaching itself (19.11b and 12b). This renders it unlikely that 'this teaching' refers to 19.9, which seems anything but optional, although some argue this on the basis of seeing a similar mollification of Jesus' hard word about wealth in 19.24–25.[15] The words translated as 'this teaching' could alternatively be translated 'this word' and refer to what the disciples had just said.[16] If so, however, the combination of the double reinforcement shifts the focus to Jesus' particular take on their comment, which removes its pessimism and applies it to some to whom it is given as gift. The saying speaks of eunuchs, men incapable of begetting children and here assumed not to marry. They were often disparaged. This is however not always the case, as in the report of the Ethiopian eunuch in Acts 8.26–40, the promise to the eunuchs as disadvantaged like sterile women in Wisdom 4.14, and its inspiration in Isaiah 56.3–5. The saying is apparently simply stating accepted fact: some are eunuchs from birth; others have been made eunuchs by castration. Rabbinic sources distinguish 'eunuchs of the sun' (born eunuchs) from 'eunuchs of man' (those either castrated or rendered eunuchs through disease): *m. Zabim* 2.1; *m. Yebamot* 8.4; *b. Yebamot* 75a 79b. Castration met with wide disapproval, and this is probably to be assumed here. Probably those born eunuchs are just taken as part of life. They may have included people whom we would call homosexual; that we cannot know. The saying may indicate awareness that not all people fit the usual categories, male and female, but need not. It shifts to a metaphorical use of eunuch when it concludes: 'there are eunuchs who have made themselves eunuchs for the sake of the kingdom of heaven'. Not all agree that this is now metaphorical. Hester argues that it does actually promote castration[17] and it may have inspired Origen's self-castration.

As a response to the disciples' pessimistic comment about whether marriage is worth entering, the statement appears to say that not doing so is, indeed, an option, but for the sake of the kingdom of heaven, not because of their pessimism. Indeed the introduction and conclusion make a point of insisting that the disciples' generalizing pessimism is to be rejected. The word 'given' refers not to whoever hears the teaching, since all might hear it, but to something God gives, something to which God calls people. Accordingly, God calls some to be eunuchs for the sake of the kingdom of heaven. Given the context, this must mean that God calls some not to marry, or remarry when that is an option. As noted in the previous chapter some relate Jesus' answer in particular to what they speculate would have been a problem with Gentiles joining Matthew's community with incestuous marriages, who must now divorce and remain unmarried;[18] but that assumes the normal pattern of declaring them invalid would not have been followed. It also shifts the focus of the saying about eunuchs from being a generalizing comment about call, and from the disciples' question, to dealing only with a few exceptional instances.

If we read it as declaring that God calls some people to remain unmarried for the sake of the kingdom of heaven, then we are still left with the question: why? Kingdom of heaven is Matthew's preferred term for kingdom of God. One might read 'for the sake of the kingdom of heaven' as meaning 'for the sake of the future kingdom of God', the age to come, that is, to live now as one will then (as in Mark 12.25; Matt. 22.30).[19] Or one could see it in very practical terms as implying that such unmarried people will be able to give more time to the work of the kingdom in the present.[20] Possibly both play a role inasmuch as the kingdom also embraces both present and future. What it does tell us is that among believers are some who are to be unmarried and some who will marry, and this is a matter of gift or calling, not of being of greater or lesser worth – or at least nothing in the context suggests this is so. Much of the language of the saying is not typical of Matthew, so that it is likely that it reflects earlier tradition.[21] A possibly independent version occurs in the writing of Justin Martyr (Justin, *Apology* 1.15.4).[22] Some, who see this as likely to have been Jesus' calling, speculate that the saying may not only derive from Jesus,[23] but even have arisen in response to criticism for his not having married,[24] pointing to the typically provocative use of the imagery of eunuchs who were considered unclean (Lev. 21.20; Deut. 23.1).[25] That is possible, but one can scarcely claim certainty. There is also a sense in which eunuchs traditionally belong in the imagery of kings and kingdoms, whose courts they often served.

Paul's preference and perspectives on celibacy

The double emphasis on this option as only for some and not for all may well indicate that Jesus or those depicting Jesus saw some danger that people might propose this for all, or even, perhaps, knew that some did. In any case it is strikingly similar to what Paul wrote to the Corinthians, where he similarly emphasizes that what in his case is a calling to celibacy is only one of two options, both of which have divine sanction: 'I wish that all were as I myself am. But each has a particular gift from God, one having one kind and another a different kind' (7.7).[26] Paul uses a different word for gift from the one used in Matthew 19.11, but the basic thought is the same. As apparently Revelation 14.4 also assumes, there are two options for believers: marrying or being unmarried. Both are God-given. Here, as probably in Matthew 19.11–12, this is being emphasized over against some who wanted to make celibacy a requirement for all.

So far we have noted notions of the future as a holy place and time without sex, and practical notions of being less encumbered and more available, as reasons why God called some to celibacy. In Paul's discussion in 1 Corinthians we meet further possible reasons. To some degree these are tangled with diverse possibilities for interpreting what Paul means at a number of points. This is so already in Paul's opening words: 'Now concerning the matters about which you wrote: "It is well for a man not to touch a woman"' (7.1). The reference to their letter and the word 'but' in 7.2 warrants NRSV's treating 'It is well for a man not to touch a woman' as a quotation from the letter, though this need not be so.[27] Then even within the statement there are uncertainties. Does 'it is well' imply that the opposite is bad, indeed sinful, or just less preferable, as 7.26? Normally an absolute demand would be expressed differently. Most agree that 'touch a woman' means have sexual intercourse as, for instance, in the Greek of Proverbs 6.29,[28] but does it mean with women in general or is it referring to one's wife? What immediately follows refers to wives and husbands, though from 7.8 Paul goes on to speak also of the unmarried. This tips the scales in favour of the more general reference.

If the saying is implying that having sexual relations with a woman, even one's wife, is sinful, then Paul cannot possibly agree, because he will go on to encourage people to do precisely that. If the saying implies that it is preferable not to have sexual intercourse with women, then assessing Paul's approach to it is more difficult. In 7.7 he is up-front about his own preference for himself and also for others, which would appear to indicate support.[29] In 7.2, however, his 'but' indicates that he can agree only with some reserve[30] and not with those wanting to say thereby that all sex is sin, something he goes out of his way to deny in 7.26 and 36.[31] This also makes it unlikely that the statement is his own, formulated to counter the lax behaviour depicted in 6.12–20, or to express concern about sex not as sin but as damaging to health, following the view of Epicurus.[32]

As we have noted in earlier chapters, Paul affirms husbands and wives 'having' each other (7.2), a probable euphemism for having sexual intercourse,[33] and grounds it with reference to the dangers of engaging in acts of sexual immorality, a theme he has just been addressing in 6.12–20, especially prostitution.[34] Some see this as the only ground, but this probably narrows Paul's meaning here. Paul is addressing married partners, so probably envisages some of them who might take 7.1 as applying also to them and so banning sex from their marriages. A realist, Paul sees this as potentially having the effect that people might as a consequence seek sexual gratification elsewhere, always a danger when sex is artificially suppressed, however pious the motivation. It is probably against those who want to ban sex from their marriages that Paul then uses the typically Stoic language of obligation and rights,[35] dangerous as that can be, although he expresses both statements in 7.2 and 7.3 in ways that do not assume unilateral action such as marital rape. It is striking that he extends this to having authority over each other's bodies (7.4). The marital emphasis continues as Paul uses the rather strong language of telling couples not to defraud or, better, deprive or cheat each other of those rights (7.5a). While Deming makes a strong case that 7.3–5 reflects Stoic discussions of marriage in their debate with Cynics, citing Antipater, Musonius, Hierocles and Plutarch, and so does not have its basis in Genesis 2.24, others emphasize biblical tradition about rights and obligations, including Exodus 21.10.[36] Satlow embraces both perspectives, observing that 'the themes and ideas that are commonly ascribed to the "Stoic–Cynic debate" were part of a common mentality in the Near East from around the turn of the Millennium and later'.[37]

It is at this point in Paul's instruction that we hear echoes of concepts of sacred space. He allows couples to stop having intercourse for a while for the sake of prayer (7.5).[38] The period of prayer is a sacred space in time, like a temple, where sex has no place. In the light of this comment it is probably to be assumed that he would not find Mark 12.25 at all strange in depicting the age to come as a place without sex, unless he shared the view that it will preserve both spaces, sacred and non-sacred. The closest parallel often cited is to be found in the *Testament of Naphtali* 8, which reads:

The commandments of the law are twofold
and to be fulfilled conscientiously.
For there is a time (for a man) to have sexual intercourse with his wife
and a time to abstain for the purpose of his prayer.
And there are two commandments;

and if they are not followed in the right order, they result in sin.
So it is also with the rest of the commandments.
Be, therefore, wise before God and prudent,
knowing the (right) order among his commandments and the
provisions relating to every matter,
so that the Lord will love you.

(8.7–10, my translation)

This extraordinary piece, possibly belonging to early Jewish material preserved in the *Testaments of the Twelve Patriarchs*, sees sexual intercourse as an aspect of love of neighbour, but sets love of God as the higher priority, and then, like Paul, sees the two as not able to occupy the same space or period of time. Deming notes that the passage may also reflect the merging of Stoic and apocalyptic thought, evident elsewhere in that work.[39]

In 7.5 Paul goes on to urge that they return to the space where sex happens, again, as in 7.2, because he does not trust the likely consequences of prolonged abstinence for married partners. Some read his following explanation, 'This I say by way of concession, not of command', as his allowing a short time of sexual abstinence for prayer,[40] or as explaining his affirmation of marriage and sex in marriage as a concession over against his preference, expressed in 7.1 and reiterated in what follows: 'I wish that all were as I myself am', that is, as someone who does not engage in sex with women (7.7a).[41] The concession could also refer not to what precedes, but to what follows in 7.7b.[42]

Paul's own preference, and to some degree his particular slant on the Corinthians' statement, then governs his advice to unmarried widowers and widows: they should remain unmarried, unless they are not managing their burning sexual passions (an image used also in Rom. 1.27; Prov. 6.27–28; Sir. 9.8b),[43] in which case marrying is better (7.8–9). Paul is not saying choose the lesser of two sins or even two evils, since he has just set out the options as divine gifts (7.7). We discussed in the previous chapter his firm but flexible application of the prohibition of divorce (7.11–15). He has already been prohibiting much more, namely the divorcing of sex from one's marriage (7.2–5). Nothing indicates that the advice to marry or not here, as opposed to later in the chapter, rests on Paul's assumptions about the shortness of time before the end[44] or that he has in mind the fires of hell.[45]

Paul's approach, which he tells us he promotes through all his churches, is that people stay put and not try to change their station

111

in life (7.17–24). We then see that he returns to apply the principle to marrying or staying unmarried. On this basis staying unmarried has nothing to do with special calling, but apparently with coping with life's dangers. In 7.26 he speaks of either an impending or a current crisis, possibly alluding to Corinth's mid-century famine.[46] Paul then tiptoes through the issues of what to do if you are tied to getting married or have been released from it (7.27).[47] His advice: stay as you are! The grounds are pragmatic: 'those who marry will experience distress' (7.28), but despite this he reassures them that if they marry that is no sin (7.28), against what the promoters of celibacy will have thought. He reinforces this pragmatic perspective with his belief that the world was soon to come to an end, and in 7.29–31 provides another nicely formulated set of contrasts to make the point he was making earlier in 7.17–24: better to stay as you are! Among these he includes: 'from now on, let even those who have wives be as though they had none' (7.29). One might take this as banning sexual intercourse after all, but in the light of 7.2–5 that cannot be so. Paul worries that the married are distracted with each other's needs, about how they might 'please' each other, probably sexually (7.32–35). Perhaps even then many would have disputed Paul's assessment, as they would today. It may well reflect the Cynic argument we find in Epictetus (late first/early second century CE) that marriage is a distraction for the wise man (Epictetus, *Discourses* 3.22.67–76; 3.24.60 and especially 4.7.5).[48] Paul probably assumes like Mark 12.25 that in the age to come there will be no such thing as sex, so it should be treated as only of transitory value. Whereas Paul describes the unmarried man as concerned with how to please the Lord, he breaks the neat parallel in depicting the virgin's and widow's concern with the affairs of the Lord, expressing it not as how they may please the Lord, but 'that they may be holy in body and spirit' (7.34). Paul reflects thereby the traditional valuing of unmarried females of his time, virgins in particular,[49] especially in relation to the holy. He may well be echoing language of his opponents.[50]

Returning to more specific issues in 7.36–38, Paul reasserts that if the sexual urges are so strong that sex 'has to be', marrying is advisable and is not a sin, but control and not marrying are better (7.36–38). The language in 7.38, about keeping her as a virgin and not marrying her, has been understood as addressing fathers about 'marrying off' their daughters, but the context makes reference to future wives more likely, though debate continues.[51] It also implies not having sex before marriage. Paul probably sees no need to undo agreements to marry which would then arise; for the new age would soon be upon them anyway, where marriage ceased to be relevant.[52] Paul's preference surfaces again on widows where he prefers them not to marry, though concedes that marriage can be appropriate if with a fellow believer ('in the Lord') (7.39–40). Wire comments that 'at the end Paul has replaced the balance of male and female with the balance of two options facing the man (7.36–8). Only at the end of the chapter does the woman receive corresponding options'.[53] In 7.39 Paul speaks of a wife being 'bound' to her husband as long as he is alive. Instone-Brewer sees this as reflecting the language of the Jewish divorce certificate, as in 7.15 and 7.22 (see also 7.27 and Rom. 7.2–3), but replacing the reference to remarrying 'only a Jew' with 'in the Lord'.[54]

Why celibacy?

Paul's qualified assertiveness ('And I think that I too have the Spirit of God') is probably countering hardline proponents of celibacy who do see entering marriage as sin and who advocate either sexual abstinence in marriage or divorce. This leaves us with two sets of questions: what drives Paul's preference for celibacy and what drives theirs? Clearly at some points Paul argues on pragmatic grounds, namely that time is short (7.29) and hardship is likely to face the married (7.26, 28b). Similarly pragmatic is his use of the argument that marriage is a distraction (7.32–35), which he justifies with a particular narrow understanding of what marriage means. Paul gives no indication of seeing marriage as an advantage in times of hardship or stress or of marrying primarily for love. It is possible to take these as the primary drivers of Paul's concerns throughout. To do so leaves gaps, however, and passes over other perspectives. Paul is also setting a higher value on restraining sexual desire than expressing it, though never painting the options as right and wrong, good and evil. The ideal of controlling passions to the extent of not only directing them rightly but suppressing their impact (7.2a, 5b, 9, 28, 36) clearly is an element in his preferring the unmarried state.

Deming draws attention to arguments between Stoics and Cynics in Paul's world about marriage and shows that Paul appears to be familiar with key terms and concepts, including notions of mutual obligation, not to speak of their shared ideal of minimizing the impact of passions, and deeming marriage a distraction. Paul differs from the Stoics in not making sex for procreation central to his argument. There are, in addition, traces of idealization of female abstinence as different from male abstinence (7.34). There is also the allusion to sacred space and time which assumes that sex and the sacred do not mix (7.5). It is also possible that a belief that the age to come, which is soon to be upon him, would be a sexless one might have helped motivate his exhortation that people stay as they are in these transitory times (7.31, 17–24, 32–34). As Newton observes, Paul 'defines sexual immorality by the use of the language of impurity'.[55] This is especially evident in his treatment of prayer in 7.5, but also behind 6.12–20; 7.14; and 7.34 (see also 1 Thess. 4.3–8; Rom. 1.24).

Thus Paul's preference appears to be not merely a matter of pragmatic choice for survival, but something spiritual, which he can describe as a gift or calling. He does, therefore, appear to share with Matthew's community the assumption that among believers there are two identifiable groups, those called to celibacy and those who marry, both expressions of divine will.

As for those whom Paul opposes, we appear to be dealing with people who are not just supporting celibacy for some but demanding it for all, or at least for those like themselves, and read the statement in 7.1 accordingly. According to Wire it was above all women prophets who were choosing this option.[56] Here, too, a number of possibilities should be considered.[57] They might, for instance, be espousing the Cynic option in the Stoic–Cynic debate about marriage[58] or ideals of suppression of passions such as Philo sees in Moses (*Life of Moses* 2.68–9).[59] They might stand under the influence of local factors in Corinth, such as applying to Christian faith celibacy practices of some of its Egyptian temples,[60] or of Jewish mysticism that spoke of marriage to heavenly Wisdom (Wisd. 8.2; Philo, *Posterity and Exile of Cain* 78)[61] or of a charismatic Pharisaism linking celibacy with prophetic gift.[62] They may have concluded that being now temples of the Holy Spirit (as in 1 Cor. 6.12–20) automatically excluded sex.[63] The snippets from the Corinthians' letter, which Paul quotes, suggest that some of Paul's own teaching is being heard/misheard and coming back to bite him, so to speak.[64] He says as much in 5.9–10. Some may even have seen his celibacy as a model – for all.[65]

Some features of the letter suggest that one possible source of misunderstanding is to be found in Paul's formulation in Galatians 3.28, which declares that 'There is no longer Jew or Greek, there is no longer slave or free, there is no longer male and female; for all of you are one in Christ Jesus.'[66] We have already noted in the discussion of 1 Corinthians 11.2–16 that some could have read the oneness as justifying the removal of what distinguishes male and female in worship and that this could be one of the reasons why, when Paul appears to repeat a similar statement about oneness in 1 Corinthians 12.13 ('For in the one Spirit we were all baptized into one body – Jews or Greeks, slaves or free – and we were all made to drink of one Spirit'), he omitted 'male and female'. Colossians similarly omits 'male and female' in its version in 3.11, perhaps out of similar concerns that some used it to promote celibacy, if that is reflected in concerns of 2.20–23.[67] The passage in 1 Corinthians 7.17–24 appears to take up the two pairs which appear in the tradition cited in Galatians 3.28 beside male and female. There could be accordingly a further reason for doing so, namely that some interpreted 'male and female' becoming one as a return to a situation where maleness and femaleness, including sexuality, no longer have a place,[68] or to an androgynous state, though usually understood as return to an original male form as Genesis presupposes and *Gospel of Thomas* 114 illustrates when it speaks of making Mary male (see also *Joseph and Aseneth* 15.1).[69] Meeks drew attention to the importance of these ideas in the world of the NT.[70] The *Gospel of Thomas* reflects a reworking of sayings of Jesus which may point in a similar direction, according to which the male and the female become one and sexual responses cease and all become as pre-puberty children (22.1–4; see also *Gospel of the Egyptians* and *2 Clement* 12.2–6).[71] This may already be envisioned in *Jubilees* 23.28–9, which speaks of a future where people live for a thousand years, all as infants and children. Such a view could then easily hear Jesus' sayings about becoming like little children or entering the kingdom as children (Mark 9.36–37; 10.14) as reflecting the same notion, namely a return to sexual innocence, perhaps connected to a return to the paradise of Eden.

There are many free-floating 'ifs' and 'buts' about such a reconstruction, but it is certainly possible that some Corinthian Christians made some of these connections and so concluded that in Christ they had left maleness and femaleness and so sexuality behind. They might also appeal to such a text as Mark 12.25, had they known it, as Balch suggests,[72] according to which celibacy is to be the destiny of all believers.[73] It is only a small step to conclude that we should therefore seek to live now as we will then, especially if they saw themselves already engaging the heavenly world, speaking in tongues of angels (1 Cor. 11.10; 13.1), and especially since in their presence sex has no place (cf. *Test. Job* 48–52).[74] Then Paul's difference with them is to some degree over issues of timing, as similarly in 1 Corinthians 4.6. Paul preferred the model which saw celibacy as something to which only some were called, the orders of creation remaining intact in the interim. Perhaps his knowledge of seriously discordant behaviour of those espousing celibacy and his appreciation of the power of passion helped strengthen his resolve to resist what he saw as their naive belief that one could live already now as if in the state of resurrection. Paul seemed to have to tackle that misconception on more than one occasion, including in accounting for his own frailty and hardship over against those who seemed to believe he should show all the signs of power and resurrection already now.

Celibacy and Jesus

Paul's preference for celibacy is unlikely to have been an innovation within the early Christian movement. Paul reports that Peter and 'the other apostles and the brothers of the Lord' were married and remained married (1 Cor. 9.5). We read of Peter's mother-in-law in Mark 1.29–31. But Paul saw celibacy as his gift and calling (1 Cor. 7.7). This was probably also the option taken by Jesus, though here opinions differ on how to interpret the silence. Phipps, for instance, mounts the case that, given that Jewish men were expected to marry and multiply (cf. Gen. 1.28), Jesus must have married; otherwise we should have heard about it as a problem.[75] Some, indeed, see the saying about eunuchs as going back to Jesus and reflecting just that: Jesus defending himself against the accusation that he had not married. It may be significant that we hear of Jesus commencing his ministry at the age of thirty (Luke 3.23), roughly the age at which men married, having accumulated enough to start a household.[76] The silence of the tradition about a wife and children is surprising, if he were married, especially in contexts which refer to his mother (and possibly father) and siblings, such as Mark 3.20–21, 31–35; 6.3, or

which name many of his women followers (Luke 8.1–3; Mark
15.40–41). Paul's listing of those married in the movement might
have included Jesus, had he, too, been married, although one could
argue in reverse, that he could have cited Jesus as being like himself,
but singleness is not really the point of his argument. Instone-Brewer
suggests that knowledge of Jesus' illegitimacy would have made finding
a wife for him difficult,[77] but this assumes a level of historical verac-
ity in the infancy narratives that they can hardly sustain.

Later Gnostic Gospels have fuelled dramatic claims that Jesus did
in fact marry and his wife was Mary Magdalene. The *Gospel of Philip*
reports that he often kissed her (55). Gnostic Gospels regularly use
sexual imagery to depict the relationship between believers and Christ,
so that even what seem to be explicit claims pointing to marriage are
probably something much less specific.[78] Mary was one of the figures,
like Judas, whom writers chose to use to claim that their revelations
came to them because of a specially favoured relationship in which
secrets were passed on, which were kept from the other disciples.
Accordingly Jesus loved her more than them (*Gospel of Mary* 10.1–3;
18.12–15; *Gospel of Philip* 55). These claims are manifestly fraudulent,
though for some in today's age they have made Jesus more humane and
accessible. Conjuring up sexual scenes by reading Jesus' instruction
to Mary Magdalene in John 20.17, not to touch or hold onto him,
as to stop having sex with him is as fanciful as interpreting foot as a
euphemism for the penis in the episode of the woman's anointing
his feet. The same is true of seeing the naked young man of Mark, let
alone of so-called Secret Mark, as indicative of sexual escapades.[79]

It seems likely that both Jesus and his predecessor John the Baptist
chose celibacy in embarking on specially prophetic tasks,[80] a connection illustrated by Anna (Luke 2.36–37) and Philip's daughters (Acts
21.8–9), as well as in Revelation (cf. 14.4) and Philo, who links it to
Moses' call (*Life of Moses* 2.68–9). This might in turn reflect influence
of the belief that prophets are especially in contact with the sacred
heavenly world where sex and its impurities have no place. John's
lifestyle in the wastelands was scarcely compatible with married life.
Living by nature's providence whether like John out there or Jesus in
Galilee was a lot easier if you were single and without family respon-
sibilities or did not acknowledge them. We also lack evidence which
would enable us to explain why they chose this lifestyle, although it
will probably have related to their stance over against the norms of

society of their day. That included challenging the power of families, including Jesus' own, and demanding that disciples be prepared to leave such interests behind.

In previous work I proposed that their stance may be very like that of the Essenes, based on their depiction in Philo, Josephus and Pliny, and the sectarian documents at Qumran, but my more recent research has shown that those documents reflect a belief system which relates sexual abstinence to sacred space (and time), and continues to see a place for sex in normal space alongside sacred space in their vision of the world to come.[81] It is therefore difficult to trace any connection between the option of John and Jesus and the alleged and probable celibacy of some Essenes, for whom it seems to have been determined by priestly concerns with holiness and special places.

Neither John the Baptist's nor Jesus' probable celibacy appears to have been taken as setting a norm or precedent. At least we have no evidence that this was the case. Neither Paul nor the Corinthian rigorists appear to have appealed to Jesus as an example. It is, however, very likely that some attached more value to this option because John and Jesus chose it. While pessimism appears in the disciples' comment in Matthew 19.10 and necessity might motivate celibacy for those needing to excise their hands and feet, and pluck out their eyes, the probable celibacy of John and Jesus and that of Paul reflects no such desperation. At the same time it does not appear to have converted into a demand among the disciples to take the celibacy option, Peter being a prime example. Having celibate men in the band of itinerant disciples may have made things easier for women to participate (Luke 8.1–2; Acts 21.9), as Witherington suggests,[82] though that might not have been unproblematic. The saying in Mark 10.29 about leaving family behind and finding hundredfold replacements mentions leaving children, but not wives. Luke's revision adds wives (18.29–30), but with no particular emphasis and probably assumes Mark's saying implied it. It is not a general rule requiring this of all, but a promise for those for whom it becomes necessary. Luke and Matthew preserve the saying which, in the case of the former, speaks of hating 'father and mother, wife and children, brothers and sisters, yes, and even life itself' (Luke 14.25–26). Other less dramatic sayings and anecdotes make it clear that the kingdom must have first priority over family (e.g. the call of the first disciples; Matt. 8.18–22; Luke 9.57–62). One could read Matthew 24.37–38 // Luke 17.26–27 as implying a negative stance toward marriage when they depict this as part of what Noah's generation were doing before the flood, but this is more likely to be attacking their carrying on with life as usual without giving heed to the warnings of Noah. On the other hand, to see marrying and being given in marriage as inappropriate, may reflect the understanding expressed in Mark 12.25; Matthew 22.30 that these cease in the age to come, and so imply that with the approach of the end they should not be pursued.[83] Mark, followed substantially by Matthew, depicts Jesus as rejecting his family's demands (3.31–35), and as noting that a prophet may not receive honour in his own house (6.4), which Luke limits to his hometown, but neither implies rejection of marriage itself or sex.

In a similar way the stories of Mary's virginity and abstinence from sexual intercourse according to Matthew during her pregnancy with Jesus seem not to have functioned as a norm. Their abstinence during pregnancy could reflect a stance sometimes espoused in Jewish literature of the time (1QapGen/1Q20 2.9–10, 13b–14a; 4QD^e/4Q270 2 ii.15–16; Josephus, *Jewish War* 161), but in the story may function simply as further reinforcement that the child could not have been Joseph's. Mary's virginity and virginal conception was after all exceptional and scarcely to be emulated.[84] On the other hand, Luke especially seems to give special attention to those who remained virgins or who as widows never remarried, the prime example being Anna the prophetess (Luke 2.36). The fact that Anna was a prophetess and that the virgin daughters of Philip were prophets (Acts 21.9) probably reflects the view that sexual abstinence might be a feature of prophets, including people like John the Baptist and Jesus.

If the depiction of the age of resurrection as one without sexual activity derives ultimately from Jesus, we find no evidence to suggest how he might have related his own celibacy to that vision, and can only speculate that he might have seen himself as already embodying the lifestyle of that kingdom in the present also in relation to sexuality, perhaps reflected in his call to be such a eunuch for the kingdom of God, but there is simply not enough evidence to know. The same perspective may have given some the sense that their calling was to live already now as they would then, but in Paul, Matthew and Revelation this appears in a way which does not disparage marriage and sex, and in the case of the former two, they go out of their way to make that clear against probable dissenters.

7

Conclusion: 'sex on the brain'?
Love and hope

Our exploration of sex in the NT has taken us down many paths. We have considered a wide range of texts and topics, including a wide range of ways of interpreting them. My assessment is that while some texts are clear, with others we have to live with considerable uncertainty. We began with same-sex relations, where Paul appears to use them like other Jews of the time, as a particularly crass instance of what happens when people turn away from the true God: for they also lose touch with their own reality and engage in unnatural sex. Also like other Jews Paul bases this judgement on what the biblical law prohibits, but also on a range of supporting arguments, which include understanding what is natural in terms of how God created things, strong disapproval of excessive sexual passion, and the shamefulness of men taking women's roles and women usurping men's. About the only argument not taken up is that such intercourse does not produce offspring. In addition Paul's descriptions do not focus on the abuse that often occurred in such relations (though no more than in heterosexual ones). Paul's assessment, like the assessment reflected in the prohibitions which he never quotes, rests on a combination of these prior assumptions, rather than on any single one.

What was deemed normal, natural and the way God made it to be appears to underlie much of what NT writers said about sexual behaviour. Sometimes any change was seen as disruptive and dangerous. Accordingly Paul insists on different attire when women and men engage in prayer and prophecy in worship and appears to limit women's teaching role. Paul assumes an order in creation which follows the sequence: God–Christ–men–women. At the same time he espouses the view that baptism celebrates oneness which transcends distinctions between male and female, Jew and Gentile, slave and free. Later in his churches we find a similar juxtaposition of commitment to hierarchical order beside an insistence that the gospel while not upsetting the order infuses it with love, which had the potential to subvert the system altogether, but would only do so many centuries later. There are, however, clear signs of subverting normal family values in what the Gospels tell us of Jesus. He modelled a lifestyle which abandoned the usual demands of family and encouraged many others to do the same for a higher priority: the kingdom of God, or one might say, the lifestyle of God. Like John before him, when he reached the usual age to marry Jesus appears to have chosen not to do so, but to remain celibate as he went about his prophetic task. Not all who joined his radical lifestyle made the same decision, as Peter shows (1 Cor. 9.5), but it was an option which Paul later followed.

It was not that there were now two value systems operating: that of the real believers who followed Jesus around, some of whom even espoused his celibate option, and that of those who remained with their families and households, who were compromised and somehow second-class. On the contrary the vision of the kingdom was just as applicable and radical for both, and included not only attitudes to wealth and the poor, but also the ways they practised marriage. At this point opinions are divided about whether Jesus forbade divorce absolutely so that Matthew's mention of adultery watered down his strictness or whether Matthew was simply spelling out what was implied all along. Certainly Jesus appears to have affirmed lifelong marriage, and almost certainly monogamous marriage. The argument he is reported as adducing to support this demand rests on the creation account of Genesis which depicts marriage as a rejoining of male and female. Like Paul, who uses the impact of sexual joining to argue against sex with prostitutes, Jesus appears to assume that sexual intercourse created something permanent which should not, therefore, be 'unjoined', broken up. Unfortunately this is the only passage we have where Jesus addresses marriage, and it serves primarily the argument about divorce. At most we can note that as in the Genesis story itself the focus is not on begetting children, but on oneness, so probably affirming the sexual intimacy of marriage. On Matthew's reading, only adultery shatters such union, and in that case Matthew appears to assume that divorce was not only warranted but mandated, as Joseph clearly presupposes, Augustan law required and Deuteronomy 24.1–4 also implied. While in practice not all would have followed this requirement, it appears to be the norm, ruling out, therefore, the kind of marriage therapy which we might apply in our day. We do not find concern expressed about individual partners and what happens to them or their children. The writers appear primarily concerned with not transgressing divine commandments.

There are some enlightening exceptions to this among the divorce sayings. Mark has Jesus speak of a man committing adultery against his wife by divorcing her and marrying another. Paul shows that in applying Jesus' divorce saying he can take other factors into account, such as the likelihood of strife where an unbelieving partner wants to end the marriage. Matthew portrays the divorcing man as forcing his wife to commit adultery (on the assumption that her best solution would be to remarry), thus wronging her by forcing her into sin and impurity (Deut. 24.1–4). This is particularly interesting because it comes in the context of Matthew's six contrasts, in which, at least in some of them, there is a strong emphasis on love for others, including one's enemy. This finds its echo later in the same collection, the Sermon on the Mount, where Jesus cites the so-called golden rule, 'In everything do to others as you would have them do to you; for this is the law and the prophets' (7.12), one of the most enlightened ethical principles of the time. Later Matthew has revised Mark's account of the question of the greatest commandment to have Jesus declare:

> 'You shall love the Lord your God with all your heart, and with all your soul, and with all your mind.' This is the greatest and first command-ment. And a second is like it: 'You shall love your neighbor as yourself.' On these two commandments hang all the law and the prophets.
>
> (22.37–40)

This raises a number of questions which can be helpful in pointing a way forward both from what is said and what is not said about sex in the NT. The first arises from the exposition of adultery in Matthew's list of six contrasts. For it shifts attention from the action to the attitude. It recognizes therefore what we noted in Chapter 1, that the most important sexual organ is not our genitalia but our brain. The same insight appears in Jesus' saying about impurities coming from within in Mark 7.21–23. The shift finds its footing also in the tenth commandment not to covet, especially in the Greek version, which can be read as: 'Do not lust after' what is not yours. What would happen, for instance, if we took 'brain adultery' into account in interpreting the divorce sayings? At first take, it would create considerable confusion, because some in their world could have read even imagining adultery as grounds for ending a marriage! It would however have the potential for directing us to the wider nexus of thoughts, feelings, attitudes and actions which make up sexual response.

A more important question still, which arises both from the prophets' depiction of Yahweh's relations with Israel and from the gospel of reconciliation through Christ, is whether God's love can make a difference to the way assumed norms are applied. The charge of adultery against Israel does not lead to permanent abandonment by God. The faith and hope of Israel rests on the assumption that there is the possibility of return and that God's compassion which confronts Israel in judgement does not evaporate. Such an understanding of God's grace is fundamental also for the way Jesus embodies restoring compassion in his ministry and Paul then reflects and interprets early Christian tradition about God's initiative in bringing reconciliation and hope to the world. While the story of Joseph and Mary presents Joseph as facing two options, public or private dismissal of Mary when he found her pregnant, and has him displaying his righteousness and compassion by choosing the kinder of the two, a broader understanding of the gospel might have led him to a third: to initiate a process of exploring reconciliation. Once you allow these broader dimensions to inform interpretation of biblical laws and social norms, the possibilities arise for greater flexibility. Paul's valuing peace in relationships (1 Cor. 7.15) is an indicator of such an approach. It also lies behind his arguments for a flexible approach to a number of matters mandated in biblical law, including circumcision and the food laws, which led him into controversy with other believers of his time, like Peter and James (e.g. Gal. 2.11–15). The same principle of the primacy of love and compassion for people underlies controversies which Jesus faced as he healed on the Sabbath and 'risked' his health by being a doctor to the sick. The application of such principles would eventually overturn the hierarchical structures of the household, with far-reaching implications in relation to slaves and women.

While there are apparent tensions between on the one hand the core insights of the gospel, which focus on transformation from inside out and reach out with unstinting grace, and on the other hand assumptions of NT writers about sexually related matters, such as adultery, divorce, gender identification and household hierarchies, it is important not to rush to resolve them or at least not to assume that *they* did. One of the most difficult and contentious tasks facing Christian faith is the way it deals with these tensions. Superficial attempts to resolve them, by giving weight to numbers of references or considering only those cases where evidence of differences survive, fail to take into account the paucity of the evidence we have for what was going on. We see, anyway, only the beginnings of attempts to resolve such tensions and the divisions which arose already in NT times. On the whole, however, unlike in the communities that produced the Dead Sea Scrolls, where differences over sex produced deep divisions, the areas of contention for the first Christians lay elsewhere than in matters of sexuality (except in Corinth), such as about circumcision, food, Sabbath observance, purity requirements and the like.

With the exception of Jesus' saying about divorce, the role of women and the apparent promotion of celibacy at Corinth, most areas relating to sexuality were not contentious. This accounts for many of the silences, such as on bestiality, rape, abortion, infanticide, castration, public nakedness and pornography, which we can surely assume they would have condemned; on contraception, on sex during menstruation, pregnancy and after childbirth, and on masturbation, which they may or may not have condemned; and on sexual use of slaves, which we hope they would have condemned. It accounts also for the normalcy which writers ascribe to household hierarchy, emphasizing female rather than male virginity, and to what makes and must end marriages, and for the deviance they see in adultery, prostitution and same-sex relations. This extends also to what they saw as appropriate for certain occasions and in certain places, where they seem to have similarly simply continued to live with traditional taboos. As sex was out of place in the Temple, so it is out of place in the period of prayer. Paul clearly assumes the occasion of worship demanded dress rules.

They apparently stood in a particular Jewish tradition which ultimately deemed sex out of place also in the age to come. Probably the image of a future where God's presence makes the whole a sacred space had the perhaps unintended consequence that sex had no future. This was not the view of most Jews, who envisaged transformation but with land and Temple, so room for sex and family, though some depictions of the future played with notions that all would be children and envisaged a return to a sacred paradise. It was then almost inevitable that some would conclude that it was more worthy to begin to live now the way one would then, especially if there was not long to go before fulfilment; but in both Paul and Matthew we see some indication of resistance against giving celibates a higher status or demanding celibacy of all.

We approach these texts as people who live a long way away from the NT world. We celebrate an end to slavery. We affirm equality of women and men. We enjoy systems of welfare and insurance which make us no longer dependent on household systems of economy. We have access to efficient contraception. We approach marriage as a complex relationship to be supported by careful preparation, planning and, where need be, therapy. We do not hold that adultery must end a marriage. We are less inclined to give special status to female virginity. We focus heavily on measuring right and wrong by the harm and good we do to others. We acknowledge that people have homosexual orientation, but differ on whether to see it as a sickness, a fruit of the fall, or a fact of life to be lived with or even celebrated. We do not silence women in church, prevent them teaching, or mandate their dress in worship. Most of us today would not assume that sexual intercourse creates a permanent bond. We are forever talking about sex – inside, outside, before and after marriage, and, in contrast to many cultures still, accept public displays of nakedness and sexual affection. In contrast to John the Baptist, we, or at least our legal jurisdictions, would see no impediment to Herod marrying his half-brother's former wife.

Yet despite this vast distance – which should never be glossed over in the interests of imagining their world as our own – most who as believers encounter these texts do so with a certain confidence that there is something permanent which addresses us from across those 2,000 years and which offers guidance and hope as we live with our sexuality. For some, that means transposing instructions and prohibitions with as little alteration as possible into the twenty-first century in the belief that this alone does them justice and fulfils obedience. For others it means weighing each instruction in the light of the whole, following the intimations of flexibility, and seeking solutions which take into account both the NT with its 2,000 years of interpreters and contemporary experience and knowledge, in the belief that this alone does justice to the texts, to people and to divine will. But even to put it like that obscures the diversity and complexities entailed in being responsible interpreters today. Despite pressures to the contrary, including from the logic of their own future expectations, the NT writers are one in seeing sex as belonging to God's creation and so as being a natural part of life to be enjoyed in the right place and the right time. They are also one in affirming the light of God's goodness which breaks through our alienation and dissemblance with love. The continuing challenge is to think these two thoughts together. This volume is not about how we might do this, but about what it is which we are interpreting and its right to be heard as far as possible in its own terms.

Notes

2 'With a man as with a woman'

1 Dan O. Via and Robert A. J. Gagnon, *Homosexuality and the Bible: Two Views* (Minneapolis: Fortress, 2003). Gagnon notes in the Acknowledgements that his contribution 'should be viewed as a revised synthesis of the *Bible and Homosexual Practice*' (ix). He also draws attention to notes which supplement his contribution, to be found in Robert A. J. Gagnon, 'Notes to Gagnon's Essay in the Gagnon-Via *Two Views* Book', <http://www.robgagnon.net/2VOnlineNotes.htm>. I cite them as Gagnon, 'Notes'.

2 In Via and Gagnon, *Homosexuality and the Bible*, 40.

3 In Via and Gagnon, *Homosexuality and the Bible*, 94.

4 In Via and Gagnon, *Homosexuality and the Bible*, 93.

5 Andrie B. du Toit, 'Paul, Homosexuality and Christian Ethics', in *Neotestamentica et Philonica: Studies in Honour of Peder Borgen* (ed. David E. Aune; Leiden: Brill, 2003), 92–107, 107.

6 The common way of abbreviating references to the Dead Sea Scrolls is as follows: in 4Q270 2 ii.16b–17a, 4 = the cave; Q = Qumran; 270 = the number of the manuscript; 2 = the fragment; ii = the column; and 16b–17a = the lines.

7 4QInstr^b/4Q416 2 iv; 4QInstr^d/4Q418 10.

8 CD 4.20–21. See William Loader, *The Dead Sea Scrolls on Sexuality: Attitudes towards Sexuality in Sectarian and Related Literature at Qumran* (Grand Rapids: Eerdmans, 2009), 107–25; also William Loader, *The Pseudepigrapha on Sexuality* (Grand Rapids: Eerdmans, forthcoming).

9 Diana M. Swancutt, '"The Disease of Effemination": The Charge of Effeminacy and the Verdict of God (Romans 1:18–2:16)', in *New Testament Masculinities* (ed. Stephen D. Moore and Janice Capel Anderson; SBLSemS 45; Atlanta: SBL, 2003), 193–234, 205–6.

10 John Nolland, 'Romans 1:26–27 and the Homosexuality Debate', *HBT* 22 (2000), 32–57, 37, 47.

11 L. William Countryman, *Dirt, Greed, and Sex: Sexual Ethics in the New Testament and Their Implications for Today* (2nd edn; Minneapolis: Fortress, 2007), 115.

12 Countryman, *Dirt, Greed, and Sex*, 114; similarly Thomas Hanks, 'Romans', in *The Queer Bible Commentary* (ed. D. Guest, R. E. Goss, M. West and T. Bohache; London: SCM Press, 2006), 582–605, 590.

13 Countryman, *Dirt, Greed, and Sex*, 110–11, 116.

14 Countryman, *Dirt, Greed, and Sex*, 109.

15 Countryman, *Dirt, Greed, and Sex*, 122; similarly Daniel Helminiak, *What the Bible* Really *Says about Homosexuality* (Millennium Edition, updated and expanded; New Mexico: Alamo Square, 2000), 77–83; Hanks, 'Romans', 586.

16 See the critical discussion in Robert A. J. Gagnon, *The Bible and Homosexual Practice: Texts and Hermeneutics* (Nashville: Abingdon, 2001), 273–7.

17 See Gagnon, *Bible and Homosexual Practice*, 247–9; Robert Jewett, *Romans* (Hermeneia; Minneapolis: Fortress, 2007), 174; Bernadette J. Brooten, *Love Between Women: Early Christian Responses to Female Homoeroticism* (Chicago: University of Chicago Press, 1998), 294–8.

18 Gagnon, *Bible and Homosexual Practice*, 251.

19 Jewett, *Romans*, 166–7.

20 So Gagnon, *Bible and Homosexual Practice*, 233; Jewett, *Romans*, 168.

21 CD 2.14—3.12. See also Loader, *Dead Sea Scrolls*, 97–107 and Jewett, *Romans*, who points to Sir. 5.2 (167).

22 Brooten, *Love Between Women*.

23 James D. G. Dunn, *Romans* (WBC 38AB; Nashville: Nelson, 1988), 64; du Toit, 'Homosexuality', 98.

24 So most recently Swancutt, 'Effemination', 209; Hanks, 'Romans', 591–2.

25 On this see William R. Schoedel, 'Same-Sex Eros: Paul and the Greco-Roman Tradition', in *Homosexuality, Science, and the 'Plain Sense' of Scripture* (ed. David L. Balch; Grand Rapids: Eerdmans, 2000), 43–72, 44–52.

26 On this see Roy Bowen Ward, 'Why Unnatural? The Tradition behind Romans 1:26–27,' *HTR* 90 (1997), 263–84, 275–76.

27 So Brooten, *Love Between Women*, 248–50 n. 99; Gagnon, 'Notes', n. 91.

28 So Gagnon, in *Homosexuality and the Bible*, 86; Schoedel, 'Same-Sex Eros', 48–9.

29 So Gagnon, *Bible and Homosexual Practice*, 272; Helminiak, *Homosexuality*, 84.

30 Jewett, *Romans*, 179.

31 Jewett, *Romans*, 179.

32 Jewett, *Romans*, 180.

33 Swancutt, 'Effemination', 211–13; Hanks, 'Romans', 598.

34 Brendan Byrne, *Romans* (SP 6; Collegeville: Liturgical Press, 1996), 70.

35 Gagnon, *Bible and Homosexual Practice*, 261–2.

36 Countryman, *Dirt, Greed, and Sex*, 114; Martti Nissinen, *Homoeroticism in the Biblical World: A Historical Perspective* (Minneapolis: Fortress, 1998), 109; Byrne, *Romans*, 77.

37 John Boswell, *Christianity, Social Tolerance, and Homosexuality: Gay People in Western Europe from the Beginning of the Christian Era to the Fourteenth Century* (Chicago: University of Chicago Press, 1980), 109.

38 Brooten, *Love Between Women*, 8–9. See also Schoedel, 'Same-Sex Eros', 55; and Mark D. Smith, 'Ancient Bisexuality and the Interpretation of Romans 1:26–27', *JAAR* 64 (1996), 223–56.

39 So du Toit, 'Homosexuality', 103–4.

40 Gagnon, in *Homosexuality and the Bible*, 81, 102.

41 Gagnon, 'Notes', n. 136.

42 Gagnon, 'Notes', n. 142.

43 Gagnon, 'Notes', n. 142.

44 E.g. Raymond F. Collins, *Sexual Ethics and the New Testament: Behavior and Belief* (New York: Crossroad, 2000), 142; du Toit, 'Homosexuality', 104; Via, in *Homosexuality and the Bible*, 16.

45 Smith, 'Ancient Bisexuality', 245; similarly Dale B. Martin, 'Heterosexism and its Interpretation of Romans 1:18–32', in Dale B. Martin, *Sex and the Single Savior: Gender and Sexuality in Biblical Interpretation* (Louisville: Westminster John Knox, 2006), 51–64, 56.

46 Via, in *Homosexuality and the Bible*, 16.

47 Robin Scroggs, *The New Testament and Homosexuality: Contextual Background for Contemporary Debate* (Philadelphia: Fortress, 1983); Hanks, 'Romans', 594.

48 Gagnon, in *Homosexuality and the Bible*, 80; Collins, *Sexual Ethics*, 144.

49 Kenneth J. Dover, *Greek Homosexuality* (London, 1978; 2nd edn, Cambridge, MA: Harvard University Press, 1989).

50 Smith, 'Ancient Bisexuality', 204 (on Dover's revised edition), 231, 237; James E. Miller, 'Response: Pederasty and Romans 1:27: A Response to Mark Smith', *JAAR* 65 (1997), 861–6, arguing pederasty remained prominent.

51 So Jewett, *Romans*, 173; John H. Elliott, 'No Kingdom of God for Softies? or, What Was Paul Really Saying? 1 Corinthians 6:9–10 in Context', *BTB* 34 (2004), 17–40, 31.

52 Gagnon, in *Homosexuality and the Bible*, 80; Gagnon, 'Notes', n. 93; Brooten, *Love Between Women*, 361.

53 Jewett, *Romans*, 180–1; exclusively: Hanks, 'Romans', 587.

54 Gagnon, in *Homosexuality and the Bible*, 79–80.

55 Gagnon, in *Homosexuality and the Bible*, 78; Gagnon, *Bible and Homosexual Practice*, 254–7.

56 Gagnon, 'Notes', n. 88, citing Craig A. Williams, *Roman Homosexuality: Ideologies of Masculinity in Classical Antiquity* (New York: Oxford University Press, 1999), 242.

57 Via, in *Homosexuality and the Bible*, 95–6.

58 Du Toit, 'Homosexuality', 100.

59 Helminiak, *Homosexuality*, 85–6.

60 Schoedel, 'Same-Sex Eros', 59, 63.

61 So Brooten, *Love Between Women*, 252.

62 So Gagnon, *Bible and Homosexual Practice*, 236.

63 Brooten, *Love Between Women*, 238, 241.

64 So Gwendolyn B. Sayler, 'Beyond the Biblical Impasse: Homosexuality through the Lens of Theological Anthropology', *Dialog* 44 (2005), 81–9, 85–6; Swancutt, 'Effemination', 194–9; Martin, 'Heterosexism', 59.

65 See Marilyn B. Skinner, *Sexuality in Greek and Roman Culture* (Oxford: Blackwell, 2005), 212–13; also Jewett, *Romans*, 176.

66 On this see Schoedel, 'Homosexuality', 50, 54, 56.

67 So Brooten, *Love Between Women*, 216.

68 Plato, *Laws* 836C; *Pseudo-Phocylides* 191.

69 Martin, 'Heterosexism', 54, 56; Boswell, *Homosexuality*, 111–14.

70 Martin, 'Heterosexism', 57–9.

71 So du Toit, 'Homosexuality', 99–100.

72 Martin, 'Heterosexism', 59; cf. J. Edward Ellis, *Paul and Ancient Views of Sexual Desire: Paul's Sexual Ethics in 1 Thessalonians 4, 1 Corinthians 7 and Romans 1* (LNTS 354; London: T&T Clark, 2007), 168–9.

73 David E. Fredrickson, 'Natural and Unnatural Use in Romans 1:24–27: Paul and the Philosophic Critique of Eros', in *Homosexuality, Science, and the 'Plain Sense' of Scripture* (ed. David L. Balch; Grand Rapids: Eerdmans, 2000), 197–222, 205–206.

74 Fredrickson, 'Natural and Unnatural Use', 217.

75 Fredrickson, 'Natural and Unnatural Use', 211.

76 Fredrickson, 'Natural and Unnatural Use', 208; see also David E. Fredrickson, 'A Friendly, Hellenic Response to Professor Sayler', *Dialog* 44 (2005), 93–4.

77 Jewett, *Romans*, 168.

78 Gagnon, *Bible and Homosexual Practice*, 178.

79 Nolland, 'Romans 1:26–27', 54; Brooten, *Love Between Women*, 275, 280; cf. Nissinen, *Homoeroticism*, 107.

80 Richard B. Hays, *The Moral Vision of the New Testament: A Contemporary Introduction to New Testament Ethics* (Edinburgh: T&T Clark, 1996), 387; Gagnon, 'Notes', 82; Gagnon, *Bible and Homosexual Practice*, 356–7; Brooten, *Love Between Women*, 269–75, 280.

81 So Nolland, 'Romans 1:26–27', 49; Gagnon, in *Homosexuality and the Bible*, 78; Gagnon, *Bible and Homosexual Practice*, 236, 290–1; Brooten, *Love Between Women*, 256.

82 Du Toit, 'Homosexuality', 101; Hays, *Moral Vision*, 386, 396; Brooten, *Love Between Women*, 275.

83 Gagnon, in *Homosexuality and the Bible*, 78.

84 Schoedel, 'Homosexuality', 57.

85 Martin, 'Heterosexism', 52; similarly Nissinen, *Homoeroticism*, 107; cf. Hays, *Moral Vision*, 384, 385, 388.

86 Gagnon, 'Notes', n. 136; Gagnon, *Bible and Homosexual Practice*, 254–6 n. 16.

87 Gagnon, 'Notes', n. 82; Gagnon, *Bible and Homosexual Practice*, 285; similarly Jewett, *Romans*, 170.

88 Gagnon, 'Notes', n. 142.

89 Brooten, *Love Between Women*, 283; Gagnon, *Bible and Homosexual Practice*, 122.

90 Gagnon, in *Homosexuality and the Bible*, 81; Brooten, *Love Between Women*, 217; du Toit, 'Homosexuality', 103; Smith, 'Ancient Bisexuality', 247.

91 Nolland, 'Romans 1:26–27', 51–2.

92 Brooten, *Love Between Women*, 282; see also Schoedel, 'Same-Sex Eros', 68.

93 Via, in *Homosexuality and the Bible*, 14.

94 Du Toit, 'Homosexuality', 100.

95 So Jewett, *Romans*, 176.

96 So Collins, *Sexual Ethics*, 132; Gagnon, in *Homosexuality and the Bible*, 76.

97 Du Toit, 'Homosexuality', 96, 98; cf. Gagnon, *Bible and Homosexual Practice*, 286.

98 On this see Elliott, 'No Kingdom of God for Softies?', 24–8; Jewett, *Romans*, 175–6; Dale B. Martin, 'Arsenokoitês and Malakos: Meaning and Consequences', in Dale B. Martin, *Sex and the Single Savior: Gender and Sexuality in Biblical Interpretation* (Louisville: Westminster John Knox, 2006), 37–50, 44–5.

99 Martin, 'Arsenokoitês and Malakos', 44.

100 Boswell, *Homosexuality*, 107, 340.

101 See the examples cited in Martin, 'Arsenokoitês and Malakos', 44–7.

102 So Gagnon, in *Homosexuality and the Bible*, 82–3; Via, in *Homosexuality and the Bible*, 'possibly if not probably correct' (12).

103 So Gagnon, in *Homosexuality and the Bible*, 82–3.

104 So Fredrickson, 'Natural and Unnatural Use', 220.

105 Boswell, *Homosexuality*, 107, 342–4.

106 *Sibylline Oracles* 2.70–7; Acts of John; Theophilus of Antioch; Hippolytus, *Refutatio* 5.26.22–3. Martin, 'Arsenokoitês and Malakos', 40–2.

107 Elliott, 'No Kingdom of God for Softies?', 29.

108 Scroggs, *New Testament and Homosexuality*, 107–8.

109 Scroggs, *New Testament and Homosexuality*, 108.

110 See David F. Wright, 'Homosexuals or Prostitutes? The Meaning of ARSENOKOITAI (1 Cor 6:9; 1 Tim 1:10)', *VC* 38 (1984), 124–53; Hays, *Moral Vision*, 382; Gagnon, in *Homosexuality and the Bible*, 67, 83; du Toit, 'Homosexuality', 94.

111 Elliott, 'No Kingdom of God for Softies?', 30.

112 Gagnon, 'Notes', n. 111.

113 So Collins, *Sexual Ethics*, 90; Elliott, 'No Kingdom of God for Softies?', 36.

114 See Countryman, *Dirt, Greed, and Sex*, 116–18.

115 See du Toit, 'Homosexuality', 94–5.

116 So Gagnon, *Bible and Homosexual Practice*, 325.

117 So Gagnon, *Bible and Homosexual Practice*, 334.

118 Scroggs, *New Testament and Homosexuality*, 119–20.

119 Gagnon, in *Homosexuality and the Bible*, 58–9.

120 Cf. Gagnon, in *Homosexuality and the Bible*, 73.

121 Gagnon, in *Homosexuality and the Bible*, 71.

122 Cf. J. David Hester, 'Eunuchs and the Postgender Jesus: Matthew 19.12 and Transgressive Sexualities', *JSNT* 28 (2005), 13–40, 37; Sayler, 'Beyond the Biblical Impasse', 83.

123 Cf. Helminiak, *Homosexuality*, 127–9. See the critique in Gagnon, 'Notes', n. 59.

124 Hanks, 'Romans', 584. Cf. Gagnon, 'Notes', n. 59.

125 Gagnon, *Bible and Homosexual Practice*, 185–7; cf. William Loader, *Sexuality and the Jesus Tradition* (Grand Rapids: Eerdmans, 2005), 21–2.

126 Loader, *Sexuality and the Jesus Tradition*, 59–60. On this see Mary J. Marshall, 'Jesus and the Banquets: An Investigation of the Early Christian Tradition concerning Jesus' Presence at Banquets with Toll Collectors and Sinners' (Diss. Murdoch University, 2002), 330–2.

127 Gagnon, *Bible and Homosexual Practice*, 191–2.

128 Gagnon, in *Homosexuality and the Bible*, 72, 75; Hays, *Moral Vision*, 383.

129 Gagnon, in *Homosexuality and the Bible*, 73; Gagnon, 'Notes', n. 33; Gagnon, *Bible and Homosexual Practice*, 105.

130 So O. Larry Yarbrough, *Not Like the Gentiles: Marriage Rules in the Letters of Paul* (SBLDS 80; Atlanta: Scholars Press, 1985), 75–6.

131 On this see Loader, *Sexuality and the Jesus Tradition*, 158–60.

3 Model marriage and the household

1 Michael L. Satlow, *Jewish Marriage in Antiquity* (Princeton: Princeton University Press, 2001), 170–3.

2 Satlow, *Jewish Marriage*, 85, referring to Num. 27.1–11; 36.1–11.

3 On this see Satlow, *Jewish Marriage*, 170–3.

4 Satlow, *Jewish Marriage*, 84; Loader, *Sexuality and the Jesus Tradition*, 48. See also the discussion of marriage practices in Loader, *Pseudepigrapha on Sexuality*, 492–4, and on Tobit, 147–85.

5 Satlow, *Jewish Marriage*, 106, 108.

6 David Instone-Brewer, *Divorce and Remarriage in the Bible: The Social and Literary Context* (Grand Rapids: Eerdmans, 2002), 3–19; Satlow, *Jewish Marriage*, 84–5.

7 Satlow, *Jewish Marriage*, 108.

8 On the archaeology of domestic dwellings see Carolyn Osiek and David L. Balch, *Families in the New Testament World: Households and House Churches* (Louisville: Westminster John Knox, 1997), 5–35.

9 Satlow, *Jewish Marriage*, 118–19.

10 Satlow, *Jewish Marriage*, 75–6.

11 Satlow, *Jewish Marriage*, 167.

12 So Robert H. Gundry, *Mark: A Commentary on His Apology for the Cross* (Grand Rapids: Eerdmans, 1993), 705.

13 So Satlow, *Jewish Marriage*, 186.

14 Loader, *Dead Sea Scrolls*, 108–19.

15 Satlow, *Jewish Marriage*, 189.

16 On this see Satlow, *Jewish Marriage*, 190–1 and William Loader, *Philo, Josephus and the Testaments on Sexuality* (Grand Rapids: Eerdmans, forthcoming).

17 William D. Davies and Dale C. Allison, *A Critical and Exegetical Commentary on the Gospel according to Saint Matthew* (3 vols; Edinburgh: T&T Clark, 1988/1991/1997), 3.18.

18 Gillian Beattie, *Women and Marriage in Paul and his Early Interpreters* (JSNTSup 296; London: T&T Clark, 2005), 102.

19 Beattie, *Women and Marriage*, 101–4.

20 Bruce W. Winter, *Roman Wives, Roman Widows* (Grand Rapids: Eerdmans, 2003), 137.

21 Dan Otto Via, *The Ethics of Mark's Gospel in the Middle of Time* (Philadelphia: Fortress, 1985), 108–11.

22 See Loader, *Dead Sea Scrolls*, 15–17, 166–7; and William Loader, *Enoch, Levi, and Jubilees on Sexuality* (Grand Rapids: Eerdmans, 2007), 275–85.

23 Raymond F. Collins, *First Corinthians* (SP 7; Collegeville: Liturgical Press, 1999), 266; similarly Countryman, *Dirt, Greed, and Sex*, 203–4.

24 Will Deming, *Paul on Marriage and Celibacy: The Hellenistic Background of 1 Corinthians 7* (2nd edn; Grand Rapids: Eerdmans, 2004), 131.

25 Yonder Moynihan Gillihan, 'Jewish Laws on Illicit Marriage, the Defilement of Offspring, and the Holiness of the Temple: A New Halakic Interpretation of 1 Corinthians 7:14', *JBL* 121 (2002), 711–44, 714–16.

26 See Loader, *Sexuality and the Jesus Tradition*, 169–71.

27 Pieter W. van der Horst, 'Sarah's Seminal Emission: Hebrews 11:11 in the Light of Ancient Embryology', in *Greeks, Romans and Christians: Essays in Honour of Abraham J. Malherbe* (ed. David L. Balch; Everett Ferguson; Wayne A. Meeks; Minneapolis: Fortress, 1990), 287–302.

28 Instone-Brewer, *Divorce and Remarriage*, 138–40.

29 Cf. Countryman, *Dirt, Greed, and Sex*, 170, 245.

30 Loader, *Sexuality and the Jesus Tradition*, 100.

31 Gagnon, in *Homosexuality and the Bible*, 71.

32 Deming, *Paul on Marriage and Celibacy*, 209, 210.

33 Dale B. Martin, 'Paul Without Passion: On Paul's Rejection of Desire in Sex and Marriage', in Dale B. Martin, *Sex and the Single Savior: Gender and Sexuality in Biblical Interpretation* (Louisville: Westminster John Knox, 2006), 65–76, 65.

34 Martin, 'Paul Without Passion', 67; See also David Fredrickson, 'Passionless Sex in 1 Thessalonians 4:4–5', *Word and World* 23 (2003), 23–30.
35 Martin, 'Paul Without Passion', 69–71.
36 Deming, *Paul on Marriage and Celibacy*, 45.
37 Ellis, *Sexual Desire*, 95. On Stoics, see pp. 96–146; in Jewish texts, pp. 18–95.
38 Osiek and Balch, *Families*, 114.
39 Deming, *Paul on Marriage and Celibacy*, 128–9.
40 Judith M. Gundry-Volf, 'Male and Female in Creation and New Creation: Interpretations of Galatians 3:28c and 1 Corinthians 7', in *To Tell the Mystery: Essays on New Testament Eschatology in Honor of Robert H. Gundry* (ed. T. E. Schmidt and M. Silva; JSNTSup 100; Sheffield: JSOT Press, 1994), 95–121, 114.
41 Gundry-Volf, 'Male and Female', 115.
42 Beattie, *Women and Marriage*, 33.
43 David L. Balch, 'Household Codes', in *Greco-Roman Literature and the New Testament: Selected Forms and Genres* (ed. D. E. Aune; SBLMS 26; Atlanta: Scholars Press, 1988), 25–50.
44 Beattie, *Women and Marriage*, 68.
45 Winter, *Roman Wives*, 167.
46 Beattie, *Women and Marriage*, 73; see also Margaret Y. MacDonald, *Colossians and Ephesians* (SP 17; Collegeville: Liturgical Press, 2000), 121.
47 Carolyn Osiek and Margaret Y. MacDonald, *A Woman's Place: House Churches in Earliest Christianity* (Minneapolis: Fortress, 2006), 33, 161–3.
48 On this see Suzanne Dixon, 'Sex and the Married Woman in Ancient Rome', in *Early Christian Families in Context: An Interdisciplinary Dialogue* (ed. David L. Balch and Carolyn Osiek; Grand Rapids: Eerdmans, 2003), 111–29.
49 So Beattie, *Women and Marriage*, 74.
50 Beattie, *Women and Marriage*, 78.
51 So Beattie, *Women and Marriage*, 77.
52 Beattie, *Women and Marriage*, 80; Osiek and MacDonald, *Woman's Place*, 126.
53 So Osiek and MacDonald, *Woman's Place*, 119–20, 122.
54 So Daniel K. Darko, *No Longer Living as the Gentiles: Differentiation and Shared Ethical Values in Ephesians 4.17—6.9* (London: T&T Clark, 2008), 84.
55 Collins, *1 Corinthians*, 265; Donald P. Senior, *1 Peter* and Daniel J. Harrington, *Jude and 2 Peter* (SP 15; Collegeville: Liturgical Press, 2003), 84.
56 Senior, *1 Peter* 82, 85; Winter, *Roman Wives*, 104, 108, 121–2; Beattie, *Women and Marriage*, 92–3.

57 Winter, *Roman Wives*, 168.
58 Osiek and MacDonald, *Woman's Place*, 103–4.
59 Osiek and MacDonald, *Woman's Place*, 117.
60 Osiek and MacDonald, *Woman's Place*, 113.
61 Benjamin Fiore, *The Pastoral Epistles: First Timothy, Second Timothy, Titus* (SP 12; Collegeville: Liturgical Press, 2007), 69.
62 Winter, *Roman Wives*, 109–12.
63 Fiore, *Pastoral Epistles*, 71.
64 See Fee, *1 Corinthians*, 699–705; Osiek and Balch, *Families*, 117.
65 Collins, *1 Corinthians*, 522.
66 Jorunn Økland, *Women in Their Place: Paul and the Corinthians Discourse of Gender and Sanctuary Space* (JSNTSup 269; London: T&T Clark, 2004), 149–51; Beattie, *Women and Marriage*, 55–6.
67 Antoinette C. Wire, *The Corinthian Women Prophets: A Reconstruction through Paul's Rhetoric* (Minneapolis: Augsburg Fortress, 1990), 155; Beattie, *Women and Marriage*, 56–9.
68 Elisabeth Schüssler Fiorenza, *In Memory of Her: A Feminist Theological Reconstruction of Christian Origins* (New York: Crossroad, 1985), 230–3.
69 Økland, *Women*, 202.
70 Økland, *Women*, 204.
71 Økland, *Women*, 204–8; see also Ben Witherington, *Women in the Earliest Churches* (SNTSMS 59; Cambridge: Cambridge University Press, 1988), 90–104.
72 Winter, *Roman Wives*, 93.
73 So Økland, *Women*, 175.
74 So Winter, *Roman Wives*, 95–6.
75 Dale B. Martin, *The Corinthian Body* (New Haven: Yale University Press, 1995), 245; Beattie, *Women and Marriage*, 49–50. See also William Loader, *Septuagint, Sexuality, and the New Testament* (Grand Rapids: Eerdmans, 2004), 27–59 on possible readings of Genesis 1—3 LXX.
76 Martin, *Corinthian Body*, 233–5, 243–5; see also Francis Watson, *Agape, Eros, Gender: Towards a Pauline Sexual Ethic* (Cambridge: Cambridge University Press, 2000), 45–50; Beattie, *Women and Marriage*, 45–6.
77 Winter, *Roman Wives*, 89–91.
78 Winter, *Roman Wives*, 81–2; Beattie, *Women and Marriage*, 46.
79 Darko, *No Longer Living as the Gentiles*, 81, challenges the idea that once egalitarian Christian households became hierarchical.
80 Wayne A. Meeks, 'The Image of the *androgyne*: Some Uses of a Symbol in Earliest Christianity', *HR* 13 (1974), 165–208, 180–9, 202, 207.
81 Martin, *Corinthian Body*, 230–2.
82 So Gundry-Volf, 'Male and Female', 107; Wire, *Corinthian Women Prophets*, 97.
83 On this see Collins, *1 Corinthians*, 397–9, 401.

84 See the discussion in Collins, *1 Corinthians*, 406–7; Anthony C. Thiselton, *The First Epistle to the Corinthians: A Commentary on the Greek Text* (NIGTC; Grand Rapids: Eerdmans; Carlisle: Paternoster, 2000), 823–6.

85 Økland, *Women*, 191.

86 Økland, *Women*, 178.

87 On these see Osiek and MacDonald, *Woman's Place*, 28.

88 See Loader, *Sexuality and the Jesus Tradition*, 39–40.

4 Adultery, attitude and disorder

1 On the Augustan laws pertaining to adultery, *Lex Iulia* and *Lex Papia Poppaea*, see Mary R. Lefkowitz and Maureen B. Fant, *Women's Life in Greece and Rome: A Source Book in Translation* (Baltimore: Johns Hopkins University Press, 1982), 181–9; and Skinner, *Sexuality*, 206–7. See also Collins, *Sexual Ethics*, 2–4; Instone-Brewer, *Divorce and Remarriage*, 9–10.

2 On this see Gail C. Streete, *The Strange Woman: Power and Sex in the Bible* (Louisville: Westminster John Knox, 1999), 76–100.

3 See n. 1 above.

4 So R. Banks, *Jesus and the Law in the Synoptic Tradition* (SNTSMS 28; Cambridge: Cambridge University Press, 1975), 217–18; R. T. France, *The Gospel of Matthew* (NICNT; Grand Rapids: Eerdmans, 2007), 179, 186.

5 France, *Matthew*, p. 187.

6 Klyne R. Snodgrass, 'Matthew and the Law', in *Treasures Old and New: Contributions to Matthean Studies* (ed. D. R. Bauer and M. A. Powell; SBLSymS 1; Atlanta: Scholars Press, 1996), 111–18; John Nolland, *The Gospel of Matthew: A Commentary on the Greek Text* (NIGTC; Grand Rapids: Eerdmans; Bletchley: Paternoster, 2005), 218–24; William Loader, *Jesus' Attitude towards the Law: A Study of the Gospels* (Grand Rapids: Eerdmans, 2002), 165–72.

7 So Hans Dieter Betz, *The Sermon on the Mount* (Hermeneia; Minneapolis: Fortress, 1995), 208, 216–17; Loader, *Jesus' Attitude towards the Law*, 172–82.

8 E.g. Paul Foster, *Community, Law and Mission in Matthew's Gospel* (WUNT 2 177; Tübingen: Mohr Siebeck, 2004), 94–5, 121–2, 141, 147, 211.

9 Anthony J. Saldarini, *Matthew's Christian–Jewish Community* (Chicago: University of Chicago Press, 1994), 125–56; Betz, *Sermon on the Mount*, 277–85; Davies and Allison, *Matthew*, 1.492; Ulrich Luz, *Matthew* (Hermeneia; 3 vols; Minneapolis: Fortress, 1989, 2001, 2005), 1.266.

10 Snodgrass, 'Matthew', 126; Warren Carter, 'Matthew's Gospel: Jewish Christianity, Christian Judaism, or Neither?' in *Jewish Christianity Reconsidered* (ed. M. Jackson-McCabe; Minneapolis: Fortress, 2007), 155–79, 166–7, 172–3.

11 E.g. Ernst Käsemann, 'The Problem of the Historical Jesus', in *Essays on New Testament Themes* (SBT 41; London: SCM Press, 1964), 15–47, here 39.

12 E.g. Countryman, *Dirt, Greed, and Sex*, 121.

13 William Loader, 'Challenged at the Boundaries: A Conservative Jesus in Mark's Tradition', *JSNT* 63 (1996), 45–61, esp. 45–51.

14 John P. Meier, *A Marginal Jew: Rethinking the Historical Jesus*, vol. 3: *Companions and Competitors* (ABRL; New York: Doubleday, 2001), 503.

15 William Loader, *Jesus and the Fundamentalism of His Day* (Grand Rapids: Eerdmans, 2001), and for greater detail, Loader, *Jesus' Attitude towards the Law*.

16 Dale C. Allison, *Jesus of Nazareth: Millenarian Prophet* (Minneapolis: Fortress, 1998), 176; Donald A. Hagner, *Matthew* (2 vols; WBC 33AB; Dallas: Word, 1993/1995), 1.120.

17 This view was widely held in the early Church, with significant consequences. Luz, *Matthew*, 1.292–3.

18 Ben Witherington, *Women in the Ministry of Jesus* (SNTSMS 51; Cambridge: Cambridge University Press, 1984), 20.

19 Betz, *Sermon on the Mount*, 233–4; Davies and Allison, *Matthew*, 1.522; Loader, *Sexuality and the Jesus Tradition*, 15.

20 Loader, *Sexuality and the Jesus Tradition*, 17.

21 Davies and Allison, *Matthew*, 1.524.

22 Betz, *Sermon on the Mount*, 238 n. 343, lists a range of Greek and Roman sources. See also Davies and Allison, *Matthew*, 1.526, who points to *m. Nid.* 2.1; see also *b. Nid.* 13a–b.

23 J. Duncan M. Derrett, 'Mark 9.42 and Comparative Legal History', in *Law in the New Testament* (Leiden: Brill, 1974), 4–31.

24 Cf. Gundry, *Mark*, 88.

25 See Derrett, 'Mark 9.42'. Josephus, *Life* 171–3; *Jewish War* 2.642–4 (cutting off the hands of rebels).

26 So Betz, *Sermon on the Mount*, 239; Collins, *Sexual Ethics*, 46.

27 So Eusebius, *Hist. Eccl.* 6.8, and Davies and Allison, *Matthew*, 1.524.

28 As Gundry, *Mark*, 524; Craig A. Evans, *Mark 8:27—16:20* (WBC 34B; Nashville: Nelson, 2001), 70.

29 Richard T. France, *The Gospel of Mark* (NIGTC; Grand Rapids: Eerdmans, 2002), 380; John R. Donahue and Daniel J. Harrington, *The Gospel of Mark* (SP 2; Collegeville: Liturgical Press, 2002), 287.

30 Loader, *Sexuality and the Jesus Tradition*, 22–4.

31 Collins, *Sexual Ethics*, 67.

32 Cf. Collins, *Sexual Ethics*, 67; Donahue and Harrington, *Mark*, 290; and Gundry, *Mark*, 525.

33 Will Deming, 'Mark 9:42—10:12, Matthew 5:27–32, and B Nid 13b: A First Century Discussion of Male Sexuality', *NTS* 36 (1990), 130–41. He refers to rabbis Eleazar, Ishmael and Tarfon.

34 See Loader, *Sexuality and the Jesus Tradition*, 24–7.
35 Loader, *Septuagint, Sexuality, and the New Testament*, 12–14 and Loader, *Philo, Josephus and the Testaments*.
36 Loader, *Sexuality and the Jesus Tradition*, 37.
37 See also Thiselton, *1 Corinthians*, 463.
38 So, for instance, Thiselton, *1 Corinthians*, 462–3; Collins, *1 Corinthians*, 243.
39 For the various attempts to define the difference see Thiselton, *1 Corinthians*, 471–3.
40 On this see Brian S. Rosner, 'Temple Prostitution in 1 Corinthians 6:12–20', *NovT* 40 (1998), 336–51, 347–8.
41 For detail see Loader, *Enoch, Levi, and Jubilees*, 91–111, 155–96; Loader, *Dead Sea Scrolls*, 356–9, and Loader, *Pseudepigrapha on Sexuality*, 490–2.
42 Satlow, *Jewish Marriage*, 262; Collins, *1 Corinthians*, 265.
43 So Frank J. Matera, *II Corinthians: A Commentary* (Louisville: Westminster John Knox, 2003), 162; Murray J. Harris, *The Second Epistle to the Corinthians: A Commentary on the Greek Text* (Grand Rapids: Eerdmans, 2005), 498.
44 Deming, *Paul on Marriage*, 216.
45 Charles A. Wanamaker, *The Epistles to the Thessalonians* (NIGTC; Grand Rapids: Eerdmans, 1990), 153; Earl Richard, *First and Second Thessalonians* (SP 11; Collegeville: Liturgical Press, 1995), 198–9.
46 Fredrickson, 'Passionless Sex', 24; Collins, *Sexual Ethics*, 104; Yarbrough, *Not Like the Gentiles*, 68–72.
47 Wanamaker, *Thessalonians*, 153.
48 See the discussion in Loader, *Dead Sea Scrolls*, 304–6.
49 So Yarbrough, *Not Like the Gentiles*, 80–1
50 So Wanamaker, *Thessalonians*, 155.
51 Collins, *Sexual Ethics*, 106; Countryman, *Dirt, Greed, and Sex*, 104; Yarbrough, *Not Like the Gentiles*, 76.
52 Fredrickson, 'Passionless Sex', 26.
53 Fredrickson, 'Passionless Sex', 27–8.
54 Richard, *Thessalonians*, 200–1.
55 Richard, *Thessalonians*, 198–9.

5 Divorce and remarriage

1 On this passage see Loader, *Sexuality and the Jesus Tradition*, 94–102.
2 Instone-Brewer, *Divorce and Remarriage*, 134–41; similarly Witherington, *Women in the Ministry of Jesus*, 24–5 and Abel Isaksson, *Marriage and Ministry in the New Temple: A Study with Special References to Mt. 19.13–22 and 1 Cor. 11.3–16* (ASNU 24; Lund: Gleerup; Copenhagen: Munksgaard, 1965), 70–1. See the critique in David R. Catchpole, 'The

Synoptic Divorce Material as a Tradition Historical Problem', *BJRL* 57 (1974), 92–127, 94–5; Davies and Allison, *Matthew*, 3.4–5.

3 David Instone-Brewer, 'Deuteronomy 24:1–4 and the Origin of the Jewish Divorce Certificate', *JJS* 49 (1998), 230–43, 231–4.

4 See the discussion in Loader, *Septuagint*, 71–6.

5 Instone-Brewer, *Divorce and Remarriage*, 28–31; and on the longer and shorter form of the *get*, pp. 117–25, including that key elements of its wording go back to the fourteenth century BCE (119).

6 On this see Instone-Brewer, *Divorce and Remarriage*, 31–2; see also Betz, *Sermon on the Mount*, 245–7.

7 On this see Instone-Brewer, *Divorce and Remarriage*, 126 n. 156, who notes the Babylonian Talmud traditions according to which the death penalty ceased soon after 30 CE (*b. Sanhedrin* 15a; *b. Sanhedrin* 41ab; *b. Abodah Zarah* 8a). See also Josephus, *Against Apion* 2.25, who asserts it; similarly, the Mishnah, *m. Sanhedrin* 7.2; 6.4; 7.3 and Philo, *On Joseph* 44. John 7.53—8.11 probably reflects a mob action.

8 On polygyny in Israel see Instone-Brewer, *Divorce and Remarriage*, 59–61.

9 So Instone-Brewer, *Divorce and Remarriage*, 54–8.

10 Davies and Allison, *Matthew*, 3.12; similarly Phillip Sigal, *The Halakhah of Jesus of Nazareth according to the Gospel of Matthew* (Atlanta: SBL, 2007), 116.

11 So David C. Jones, 'A Note on the LXX of Malachi 2.16', *JBL* 109 (1990), 683–5.

12 See Loader, *Dead Sea Scrolls*, 107–19; Instone-Brewer, *Divorce and Remarriage*, 61–72.

13 See the detailed discussion in Instone-Brewer, *Divorce and Remarriage*, 110–17.

14 Instone-Brewer, *Divorce and Remarriage*, 24–6, 72–80, 85–90 and Satlow, *Jewish Marriage*, 214.

15 Satlow, *Jewish Marriage*, 214.

16 See Instone-Brewer, *Divorce and Remarriage*, 75–80.

17 Instone-Brewer, *Divorce and Remarriage*, 87–8.

18 Instone-Brewer, *Divorce and Remarriage*, 72–3, 190–1.

19 Satlow, *Jewish Marriage*, 214.

20 So Gundry, *Mark*, 538.

21 Instone-Brewer, *Divorce and Remarriage*, 144–6.

22 Davies and Allison, *Matthew*, 3.14–15; Loader, *Sexuality and the Jesus Tradition*, 98.

23 So E. P. Sanders, *Jesus and Judaism* (London: SCM Press, 1985), 259; Gundry, *Mark*, 540; cf. Hays, *Moral Vision*, 351.

24 Anthony E. Harvey, 'Genesis versus Deuteronomy? Jesus on Marriage and Divorce', in *The Gospels and the Scriptures of Israel* (ed. C. A. Evans and W. R. Stegner; JSNTSup 104/Studies in Scripture in Early Judaism and Christianity 3; Sheffield: JSOT Press, 1994), 55–65, 56.

25 On this see Loader, *Septuagint*, 27–42.
26 On this see Deming, *Paul on Marriage and Celibacy*, 143.
27 See Loader, *Sexuality and the Jesus Tradition*, 95, 97; Loader, *Jesus' Attitude towards the Law*, 39–55, 518–19.
28 So Sanders, *Jesus and Judaism*, 256–7, who helped shape our broader understanding of Jewish Law. See also John P. Meier, *A Marginal Jew: Rethinking the Historical Jesus*, vol. 4: *Law and Love* (New Haven: Yale University Press, 2009), who writes: 'It is nonsense to speak of the Jewish Jesus abrogating or annulling the Mosaic Law' (126), while at the same time noting the jarring nature of Jesus' assertion.
29 See Loader, *Sexuality and the Jesus Tradition*, 102–7.
30 So Instone-Brewer, *Divorce and Remarriage*, 134–5.
31 So Instone-Brewer, *Divorce and Remarriage*, 142–4, 171–5; Hays, *Moral Vision*, 350; Gundry, *Mark*, 530.
32 So cf. Catchpole, 'Synoptic Divorce Material', 115–16; Loader, *Sexuality and the Jesus Tradition*, 105.
33 So Hays, *Moral Vision*, 352; similarly Via, *Ethics of Mark's Gospel*, 112.
34 So Craig L. Blomberg, 'Marriage, Divorce, Remarriage, and Celibacy: An Exegesis of Matthew 19.3–12', *TJ* 11 (1990), 161–96, 175; Joseph A. Fitzmyer, 'The Matthean Divorce Texts and Some New Palestinian Evidence', in *To Advance the Gospel: New Testament Studies* (2nd edn; Grand Rapids: Eerdmans, 1998), 79–111 on Matt. 5.32 (87).
35 So Gundry, *Mark*, 532 and 541–2; John Nolland, 'The Gospel Prohibition of Divorce: Tradition History and Meaning', *JSNT* 58 (1995), 19–35, 28–9.
36 Hays, *Moral Vision*, 351; see also Instone-Brewer, *Divorce and Remarriage*, 151.
37 So Gundry, *Mark*, 533; Fitzmyer, 'Matthean Divorce Texts', 85.
38 On this see Dixon, 'Sex and the Married Woman'.
39 So Bruce Metzger, *A Textual Commentary on the Greek New Testament* (2nd edn; London and New York: United Bible Societies, 1994). Nolland, *Matthew*, explains the different exception clause in 19.9 as Matthew's attempt to link the saying more closely to the Genesis texts than to Deuteronomy (775).
40 Betz, *Sermon on the Mount*, 249; Instone-Brewer, *Divorce and Remarriage*, who maintains that rabbinic tradition saw remarriage after invalid divorce as adultery (125–32).
41 So Davies and Allison, *Matthew*, 1.528, pointing also to the plight of widows (Ruth 1.20–21; Ps. 94.6; Isa. 1.23; 10.2; 54.4).
42 Isaksson, *Marriage and Ministry*, 147.
43 Davies and Allison, *Matthew*, 1.532; Luz, *Matthew*, 1.307; Hagner, *Matthew*, 1.123; Betz, *Sermon on the Mount*, 251.
44 Alan Watson, 'Jesus and the Adulteress', *Bib* 80 (1999), 100–8.
45 Harvey, 'Genesis versus Deuteronomy?', 64–5.

46 Sigal, *Halakhah*, 119; Luz, *Matthew*, 1.304–6; Davies and Allison, *Matthew*, 3.16; Blomberg, 'Marriage, Divorce, Remarriage', 177–8; France, *Matthew*, 209.

47 Thus adultery and indecency; so Betz, *Sermon on the Mount*, 250; Hays, *Moral Vision*, 354–5.

48 Countryman, *Dirt, Greed, and Sex*, 170–1; Fitzmyer, 'Matthean Divorce Texts', 88.

49 So Davies and Allison, *Matthew*, 1.529–31.

50 So Davies and Allison, *Matthew*, 1.529–31; Luz, *Matthew*, 1.304–6; Hagner, *Matthew*, 1.124–5; Stephen C. Barton, *Discipleship and Family Ties in Mark and Matthew* (SNTSMS 80; Cambridge: Cambridge University Press, 1994), 196–7; Blomberg, 'Marriage, Divorce, Remarriage', 177.

51 So Isaksson, *Marriage*, 116–52; Countryman, *Dirt, Greed, and Sex*, 170–1.

52 Davies and Allison, *Matthew*, 1.529; see also Luz, *Matthew*, 1.304–6; Blomberg, 'Marriage, Divorce, Remarriage', 176.

53 Francis J. Moloney, 'Matthew 19:3–12 and Celibacy', in *'A Hard Saying': The Gospel and Culture* (Collegeville: Liturgical Press, 2001), 35–52, esp. 38–9; Fitzmyer, 'Matthean Divorce Texts', 88–9; Ben Witherington, 'Matthew 5.32 and 19.9 – Exception or Exceptional Situation', *NTS* 31 (1985), 571–6.

54 Fitzmyer, 'Matthean Divorce Texts', 89.

55 Fitzmyer, 'Matthean Divorce Texts', 89.

56 Fitzmyer, 'Matthean Divorce Texts', 91–7.

57 Instone-Brewer, *Divorce and Remarriage*, 157–8.

58 Davies and Allison, *Matthew*, 1.529–31.

59 So Banks, *Jesus and the Law*, 155–9; cf. Betz, *Sermon on the Mount*, 250.

60 So Markus Bockmuehl, 'Matthew 5.32; 19.9 in the Light of Pre-Rabbinic Halakah', *NTS* 35 (1989), 291–95, here 292; *Matthew*, on 19.9. See also Instone-Brewer, *Divorce and Remarriage*, 153, 159.

61 Betz, *Sermon on the Mount*, 250.

62 Instone-Brewer, *Divorce and Remarriage*, 152–9; a view I also once espoused in Loader, *Jesus' Attitude towards the Law*, 225. Similarly Saldarini, *Matthew's Christian–Jewish Community*, 150; Davies and Allison, *Matthew*, 1.530; France, *Matthew*, 209.

63 On this see Loader, *Sexuality and the Jesus Tradition*, 106–7.

64 On this see France, *Matthew*, 208, 210.

65 Instone-Brewer, *Divorce and Remarriage*, 152–63; similarly France, *Matthew* 211.

66 Instone-Brewer, *Divorce and Remarriage*, 184–5. See the discussion in Loader, *Sexuality and the Jesus Tradition*, 119–20.

67 Nolland, 'Gospel Prohibition of Divorce', 33.

68 See Loader, *Sexuality and the Jesus Tradition*, 83–8.

69 Nolland, 'Gospel Prohibition of Divorce', 31; but see the critique of Frans Neirynck, 'The Sayings of Jesus in 1 Corinthians', in *The Corinthian Correspondence* (ed. R. Bieringer; BETL 125; Leuven: Peeters, 1996), 141–76, here 170–1.

70 On this see Fitzmyer, 'Matthean Divorce Texts', 81; Countryman, *Dirt, Greed, and Sex*, 322 n. 24.

71 So Neirynck, 'Sayings of Jesus', 161; Raymond F. Collins, *Divorce in the New Testament* (Collegeville: Liturgical Press, 1992), 15–22; Fee, *1 Corinthians*, 293.

72 So Fee, *1 Corinthians*, 296.

73 So J. Dorcas Gordon, *Sister or Wife? 1 Corinthians 7 and Cultural Anthropology* (JSNTSup 149; Sheffield: JSOT Press, 1997), 118. Collins, *Divorce*, 23–4; Collins, *1 Corinthians*, 264, 269.

74 So Wire, *Corinthian Women Prophets*, 84; similarly Neirynck, 'Sayings of Jesus', 163–4.

75 So Catchpole, 'Synoptic Divorce Material', 110; Neirynck, 'Sayings of Jesus', 167–8; Countryman, *Dirt, Greed, and Sex*, 202.

76 So Wire, *Corinthian Women Prophets*, 84–5; Gordon, *Sister or Wife?*, 115–18; Gundry-Volf, 'Male and Female', 118 n. 70.

77 So Fee, *1 Corinthians*, 295.

78 Collins, *1 Corinthians*, 269.

79 Wire, *Corinthian Women Prophets*, 79.

80 So Instone-Brewer, *Divorce and Remarriage*, 202.

81 Dale C. Allison, 'Divorce, Celibacy, and Joseph', *JSNT* 49 (1993), 3–10, 5.

82 Similarly Gundry, *Mark*, 536–7; Catchpole, 'Synoptic Divorce Material', 114–15; Fitzmyer, 'Matthean Divorce Texts', 98; Loader, *Sexuality and the Jesus Tradition*, 108–11.

83 See the discussion in Luz, *Matthew*, 1.302–3, 306; Fitzmyer, 'Matthean Divorce Texts', 99–100; cf. Walter Wink, *Engaging the Powers* (Minneapolis: Fortress, 1992), 132; Countryman, *Dirt, Greed, and Sex*, 183; William E. Phipps, *The Sexuality of Jesus: Theological and Literary Perspectives* (New York, Harper & Row, 1993), 50.

84 So Hays, *Moral Vision*, 357; Davies and Allison, *Matthew*, 3.17.

85 So Blomberg, 'Marriage, Divorce, Remarriage', 181; similarly Nolland, 'Gospel Prohibition of Divorce'; cf. Hagner, *Matthew*, 2.549.

86 Fitzmyer, 'Matthean Divorce Texts', 85.

6 Has sex a future? The question of celibacy

1 J. Harold Ellens, *Sex in the Bible: A New Consideration* (Psychology, Religion, and Spirituality; Westport: Praeger, 2008), 46.

2 Cf. Witherington, *Women in the Ministry of Jesus*, 32–5.

3 Cf. Schüssler Fiorenza, *In Memory of Her*, 143–5.

4 For further detail see Loader, *Sexuality and the Jesus Tradition*, 121–6.

5 So Gundry, *Mark*, 706; Luz, *Matthew*, on 22.30.

6 Allison, *Jesus*, 177.

7 On this see Loader, *Enoch, Levi, and Jubilees*, 8–52.

8 Streete, *Strange Woman*, 9.

9 Osiek and Balch, *Families*, 152–3.

10 For what follows see Loader, *Dead Sea Scrolls*, 376–83.

11 Stephen Mason, 'What Josephus Says About the Essenes in his Judean War', in *Text and Artifact in the Religions of Mediterranean Antiquity: Essays in Honour of Peter Richardson* (ed. S. Wilson and M. Desjardins; Waterloo, Ont.: Wilfrid Laurier University Press, 2000), 423–55, 426. See Loader, *Dead Sea Scrolls*, 369–74.

12 See Loader, *Enoch, Levi, and Jubilees*, 236–45.

13 Daniel C. Olson, ' "Those who have not defiled themselves with women": Revelation 14.4 and the Book of Enoch', *CBQ* 59 (1997), 492–510, 496–7, 502–5.

14 David E. Aune, *Revelation* (3 vols; WBC 52; Nashville: Thomas Nelson, 1998), 2.810.

15 So Quenton Quesnell, ' "Made themselves Eunuchs for the Kingdom of Heaven" (Mt 19:12)', *CBQ* 30 (1968), 335–58; Moloney, 'Matthew 19:3–12 and Celibacy', 42.

16 So Davies and Allison, *Matthew*, 3.20–1; Blomberg, 'Marriage, Divorce, Remarriage', 84; France, *Matthew*, 723; Nolland, *Matthew*, 776.

17 Hester, 'Eunuchs', 30.

18 Fitzmyer, 'Matthean Divorce Texts', 89; Moloney, 'Matthew 19:3–12 and Celibacy', 38–9.

19 Luz, *Matthew*, on 2.30; Witherington, *Women in the Ministry of Jesus*, 31.

20 So Jerome Kodell, 'The Celibacy Logion in Matthew 19:12', *BTB* 8.1 (1978), 19–23, 21.

21 So Davies and Allison, *Matthew*, 3.19–20.

22 So Joseph Blinzler, 'Justinus Apol. I 15,4 und Matthäus 19,10–12', in *Melanges Bibliques en hommage au R. Beda Rigaux* (ed. A. Descamps and R. P. Andre de Halleux; Gembloux: Ducolot, 1970), 45–55, but see the discussion in Luz, *Matthew*, on 19.11–12; Davies and Allison, *Matthew*, 3.20.

23 So Luz, *Matthew*, on 19.11–12; Witherington, *Women in the Ministry of Jesus*, 12; Pieter W. van der Horst, 'Celibacy in Early Judaism', *RB* 109 (2002), 390–402, here 398.

24 Moloney, 'Matthew 19:3–12 and Celibacy', 46–52; Luz, *Matthew*, on 19.11–12.

25 So Witherington, *Women in the Ministry of Jesus*, 30; Davies and Allison, *Matthew*, 3.24 n. 122; cf. Phipps, *Sexuality of Jesus*, arguing the opposite on the same basis (47).

26 Davies and Allison, *Matthew*, 3.24.

27 Cf. Chrys C. Caragounis, '"Fornication" and "Concession"? Interpreting 1 Cor 7,1–7', in *The Corinthian Correspondence* (ed. R. Bieringer; BETL 125; Leuven: Peeters, 1996), 543–60, 545 n. 2, 559.

28 Fee, *1 Corinthians*, 275; Thiselton, *1 Corinthians*, 500; Gordon D. Fee, '1 Corinthians 7:1–7 Revisited', in *Paul and the Corinthians: Studies on a Community in Conflict: Essays in Honour of Margaret Thrall* (ed. Trevor J. Burke and J. Keith Elliott; NovTSup 109; Leiden: Brill, 2003), 197–213, disputing Caragounis, '"Fornication" and "Concession"?' and the reply in Chrys C. Caragounis, 'What Did Paul Mean? The Debate on 1 Cor 7,1–7', *ETL* 82 (2006), 187–97.

29 Countryman, *Dirt, Greed, and Sex*, 322 n. 18.

30 Fee, *1 Corinthians*, 274; Wire, *Corinthian Women Prophets*, 80; Gundry-Volf, 'Controlling the Bodies: A Theological Profile of the Corinthian Sexual Ascetics (1 Cor 7)', in *The Corinthian Correspondence* (ed. R. Bieringer; BETL 125; Leuven: Peeters, 1996), 519–41, 525.

31 So Thiselton, *1 Corinthians*, 498–500; Fee, *1 Corinthians*, 332–3; Gundry-Volf, 'Controlling the Bodies', 522; Collins, *1 Corinthians*, 252–3, 257–8.

32 On this see Osiek and Balch, *Families*, 114.

33 Collins, *1 Corinthians*, 258; Hays, *Moral Vision*, 48; Fee, *1 Corinthians*, 278–9.

34 So Fee, *1 Corinthians*, 278; Norbert Baumert, *Woman and Man in Paul: Overcoming a Misunderstanding* (Collegeville: Liturgical Press, 1996), 32–3.

35 On this see Deming, *Paul on Marriage and Celibacy*, 113–15.

36 Brian S. Rosner, *Paul, Scripture and Ethics: A Study of 1 Corinthians 5–7* (AGJU 22; Leiden: Brill, 1994), 159–60; Instone-Brewer, *Divorce and Remarriage*, 99–110. See also Countryman, *Dirt, Greed, and Sex*, 144–63.

37 Satlow, *Jewish Marriage*, 39.

38 On this see Gundry-Volf, 'Controlling the Bodies', 530–1, 531.

39 Deming, *Paul on Marriage and Celibacy*, 120–3.

40 Fee, *1 Corinthians*, 284; Hays, *Moral Vision*, 50; Thiselton, *1 Corinthians*, 510–11.

41 Caragounis, '"Fornication" and "Concession"?', suggests that the word may not mean 'concession', but 'pardon' for discussing intimate things 555–9.

42 So Bruce Winter, '1 Corinthians 7:6–7: A Caveat and a Framework for "The Sayings" in 7:8–24', *TynBul* 48 (1997), 57–65; Baumert, *Woman and Man in Paul*, 44–6.

43 On this see Deming, *Paul on Marriage and Celibacy*, 128–9; Thiselton, *1 Corinthians*, 518.

44 Cf. Countryman, *Dirt, Greed, and Sex*, 200; Hays, *Moral Vision*, 51–2.

45 Cf. Osiek and Balch, *Families*, 114.

46 So Bruce Winter, 'Secular and Christian Responses to Corinthian Famines', *TynBul* 40 (1989), 86–106.

47 See Fee, *1 Corinthians*, 326–7.

48 On this see Fee, *1 Corinthians*, 340; Collins, *1 Corinthians*, 291; Deming, *Paul on Marriage and Celibacy*, affirming Paul's affinity to Stoics who espoused Cynic stances (194–5), rather than echoing Stoic *apatheia* as suggested by Vincent L. Wimbush, *Paul, the Worldly Ascetic: Response to the World and Self-Understanding according to 1 Corinthians 7* (Macon: Mercer University Press, 1987), 50–62, and David L. Balch, '1 Cor 7.32–35 and Stoic Debates about Marriage, Anxiety, and Distraction', *JBL* 102 (1983), 428–39.

49 On virginity as prized in the Mediterranean and the Near East see Satlow, *Jewish Marriage*, 118–19.

50 So Gordon, *Sister or Wife?*, 129; Gundry-Volf, 'Controlling the Bodies', 534–5; Collins, *1 Corinthians*, 292.

51 See Thiselton, *1 Corinthians*, 597–8; Fee, *1 Corinthians*, 326; and Chrys C. Caragounis, *The Development of Greek and the New Testament: Morphology, Syntax, Phonology, and Textual Transmission* (Grand Rapids: Baker, 2006), 299–316, who argues that it refers to man's handling of his own virginity.

52 See Loader, *Sexuality and the Jesus Tradition*, 181.

53 Wire, *Corinthian Women Prophets*, 89.

54 So Instone-Brewer, *Divorce and Remarriage*, 28–31, 122, 202–3.

55 Michael Newton, *The Concept of Purity at Qumran and in the Letters of Paul* (SNTSMS 53; Cambridge: Cambridge University Press, 1985), 102–9, 102; similarly John C. Poirier and Joseph Frankovic, 'Celibacy and Charism in 1 Cor 7:5–7', *HTR* 89 (1996), 1–18, 4.

56 Wire, *Corinthian Women Prophets*, 97; similarly Gordon, *Sister or Wife?*, 110–11, 118–91.

57 See also Deming, *Paul on Marriage and Celibacy*, 1–46 and Gundry-Volf, 'Controlling the Bodies', 519–20; Thiselton, *1 Corinthians*, 487–93.

58 Deming, *Paul on Marriage and Celibacy*, 3, 107–27, 208.

59 David L. Balch, 'Backgrounds of 1 Cor. vii: Sayings of the Lord in Q: Moses as an ascetic THEIOS ANHR in II Cor. iii.', *NTS* 18 (1971/2), 351–64, 355–64.

60 Richard E. Oster, 'Use, Misuse and Neglect of Archaeological Evidence in Some Modern Works on 1 Corinthians (1 Cor 7,1–5; 8,10; 11,2–16; 12,14–26)', *ZNW* 83 (1992), 52–73, 60–4; see also Collins, *1 Corinthians*, 253.

61 Richard A. Horsley, 'Spiritual Marriage with Sophia', *VC* 33 (1979), 32–7.

62 Poirier and Frankovic, 'Celibacy and Charism', 11, 14–17.

63 Gundry-Volf, 'Controlling the Bodies', 519–20, 536–7; see also Wire, *Corinthian Women Prophets*, 90.

64 So John C. Hurd, *The Origin of 1 Corinthians* (Macon: Mercer University Press, 1983; originally London: SPCK, 1965), 275; similarly Yarbrough, *Not Like the Gentiles*, 121.

65 Deming, *Paul on Marriage and Celibacy*, 125; Collins, *1 Corinthians*, 256.

66 So Gundry-Volf, 'Male and Female', 100.

67 On this see MacDonald, *Colossians and Ephesians*, 116, 121.

68 Dennis R. MacDonald, *There is No Male and Female: The Fate of a Dominical Saying in Paul and Gnosticism* (Philadelphia: Fortress, 1987), 98–102; MacDonald, 'Women Holy in Body and Spirit', 166; Gundry-Volf, 'Male and Female', 95–121.

69 See also Martin, *Corinthian Body*, 230–2.

70 Meeks, 'Image of the *Androgyne*', 180–9, 202, 207. See the critical discussion in Gundry-Volf, 'Male and Female', 102–4.

71 See Loader, *Sexuality and the Jesus Tradition*, 199–207. See also van der Horst, 'Celibacy in Early Judaism', 399 n. 32; Amy-Jill Levine, 'The Word Becomes Flesh: Jesus, Gender, and Sexuality', in *Jesus Two Thousand Years Later* (ed. James H. Charlesworth; Harrisburg: Trinity Press International, 2000), 62–83, 76; J. Dominic Crossan, *The Historical Jesus: The Life of a Mediterranean Jewish Peasant* (San Francisco: Harper, 1991), 267.

72 Balch, 'Backgrounds of 1 Cor. vii', 353–5.

73 See also Hurd, *Origin of 1 Corinthians*, 276–7; MacDonald, *Male and Female*, 71; Gordon, *Sister or Wife?*, 131 n. 110.

74 See Yarbrough, *Not Like the Gentiles*, 118–20; David R. Cartlidge, '1 Corinthians 7 as a Foundation for a Christian Sex Ethic', *JR* 55 (1975), 220–34, 227, 229–30.

75 Phipps, *Sexuality of Jesus*, 40–1.

76 Satlow, *Jewish Marriage*, 108–9.

77 Instone-Brewer, *Divorce and Remarriage*, 169.

78 On this see Majella Franzmann, *Jesus in the Nag Hammadi Writings* (Edinburgh: T&T Clark, 1996), 130.

79 Cf. Morton Smith, *The Secret Gospel: The Discovery and Interpretation of the Secret Gospel according to Mark* (New York: Harper & Row, 1973), 17.

80 Poirier and Frankovic, 'Celibacy and Charism', 11–18. See also Geza Vermes, *Jesus the Jew: A Historian's Reading of the Gospels* (London: Collins, 1973), 99–102; van der Horst, 'Celibacy in Early Judaism', 396–8.

81 Loader, *Dead Sea Scrolls*, 369–83; cf. Loader, *Sexuality and the Jesus Tradition*, 217–18.

82 Witherington, *Women in the Ministry of Jesus*, 31–2.

83 See Loader, *Sexuality and the Jesus Tradition*, 141.

84 On this see Loader, *Sexuality and the Jesus Tradition*, 208–9.

Bibliography

Allison, Dale C., *Jesus of Nazareth: Millenarian Prophet* (Minneapolis: Fortress, 1998)

Aune, David E., *Revelation* (3 vols; WBC 52; Nashville: Thomas Nelson, 1998)

Balch, David L., '1 Cor 7:32–35 and Stoic Debates about Marriage, Anxiety, and Distraction', *JBL* 102 (1983), 428–39

Balch, David L., 'Backgrounds of 1 Cor. vii: Sayings of the Lord in Q: Moses as an ascetic THEIOS ANHR in II Cor. iii.', *NTS* 18 (1971/2), 351–64

Balch, David L., 'Household Codes', in *Greco-Roman Literature and the New Testament: Selected Forms and Genres* (ed. D. E. Aune; SBLMS 26; Atlanta: Scholars Press, 1988), 25–50

Balch, David L. and Osiek, Carolyn, eds, *Early Christian Families in Context: An Interdisciplinary Dialogue* (Grand Rapids: Eerdmans, 2003)

Banks, Robert, *Jesus and the Law in the Synoptic Tradition* (SNTSMS 28; Cambridge: Cambridge University Press, 1975)

Barton, Stephen C., *Discipleship and Family Ties in Mark and Matthew* (SNTSMS 80; Cambridge: Cambridge University Press, 1994)

Baumert, Norbert, *Woman and Man in Paul: Overcoming a Misunderstanding* (Collegeville: Liturgical Press, 1996)

Beattie, Gillian, *Women and Marriage in Paul and his Early Interpreters* (JSNTSup 296; London: T&T Clark, 2005)

Betz, Hans Dieter, *The Sermon on the Mount* (Hermeneia; Minneapolis: Fortress, 1995)

Blinzler, Joseph, 'Justinus Apol. I 15,4 und Matthäus 19,10–12', in *Melanges Bibliques en hommage au R. Beda Rigaux* (ed. A. Descamps and R. P. Andre de Halleux; Gembloux: Ducolot, 1970), 45–55

Blomberg, Craig L., 'Marriage, Divorce, Remarriage, and Celibacy: An Exegesis of Matthew 19.3–12', *TJ* 11 (1990), 161–96

Bockmuehl, Markus, 'Matthew 5.32; 19.9 in the Light of Pre-Rabbinic Halakah', *NTS* 35 (1989), 291–5

Boswell, John, *Christianity, Social Tolerance, and Homosexuality: Gay People in Western Europe from the Beginning of the Christian Era to the Fourteenth Century* (Chicago: University of Chicago Press, 1980)

Brooten, Bernadette J., *Love Between Women: Early Christian Responses to Female Homoeroticism* (Chicago: University of Chicago Press, 1998)

Byrne, Brendan, *Romans* (SP 6; Collegeville: Liturgical Press, 1996)

Caragounis, Chrys C., *The Development of Greek and the New Testament: Morphology, Syntax, Phonology, and Textual Transmission* (Grand Rapids: Baker, 2006)

Caragounis, Chrys C., '"Fornication" and "Concession"? Interpreting 1 Cor 7,1–7', in *The Corinthian Correspondence* (ed. R. Bieringer; BETL 125; Leuven: Peeters, 1996), 543–60

Caragounis, Chrys C., 'What Did Paul Mean? The Debate on 1 Cor 7,1–7', *ETL* 82 (2006), 187–97

Carter, Warren, 'Matthew's Gospel: Jewish Christianity, Christian Judaism, or Neither?' in *Jewish Christianity Reconsidered* (ed. M. Jackson-McCabe; Minneapolis: Fortress, 2007), 155–79

Cartlidge, David R., '1 Corinthians 7 as a Foundation for a Christian Sex Ethic', *JR* 55 (1975), 220–34

Catchpole, David R., 'The Synoptic Divorce Material as a Tradition Historical Problem', *BJRL* 57 (1974), 92–127

Collins, Raymond F., *Divorce in the New Testament* (Collegeville: Liturgical Press, 1992)

Collins, Raymond F., *First Corinthians* (SP 7; Collegeville: Liturgical Press, 1999)

Collins, Raymond F., *Sexual Ethics and the New Testament: Behavior and Belief* (New York: Crossroad, 2000)

Countryman, L. William, *Dirt, Greed, and Sex: Sexual Ethics in the New Testament and Their Implications for Today* (2nd edn; Minneapolis: Fortress, 2007)

Crossan, J. Dominic, *The Historical Jesus: The Life of a Mediterranean Jewish Peasant* (San Francisco: Harper, 1991)

Darko, Daniel K., *No Longer Living as the Gentiles: Differentiation and Shared Ethical Values in Ephesians 4.17–6.9* (London: T&T Clark, 2008)

Davies, William D. and Allison, Dale C., *A Critical and Exegetical Commentary on the Gospel according to Saint Matthew* (3 vols; Edinburgh: T&T Clark, 1988/1991/1997)

Deming, Will, 'Mark 9:42—10:12, Matthew 5:27–32, and B Nid 13b: A First Century Discussion of Male Sexuality', *NTS* 36 (1990), 130–41

Deming, Will, *Paul on Marriage and Celibacy: The Hellenistic Background of 1 Corinthians 7* (2nd edn; Grand Rapids: Eerdmans, 2004)

Derrett, J. Duncan M., 'Mark 9.42 and Comparative Legal History', in *Law in the New Testament* (Leiden: Brill, 1974), 4–31

Dixon, Suzanne, 'Sex and the Married Woman in Ancient Rome', in *Early Christian Families in Context: An Interdisciplinary Dialogue* (ed. David L. Balch and Carolyn Osiek; Grand Rapids: Eerdmans, 2003), 111–29

Donahue, John R. and Harrington, Daniel J., *The Gospel of Mark* (SP 2; Collegeville: Liturgical Press, 2002)

Dover, Kenneth J., *Greek Homosexuality* (London, 1978; 2nd edn; Cambridge, MA: Harvard University Press, 1989)

Dunn, James D. G., *Romans* (WBC 38AB; Nashville: Nelson, 1988)

Ellens, J. Harold, *Sex in the Bible: A New Consideration* (Psychology, Religion, and Spirituality; Westport: Praeger, 2008)

Elliott, John H., 'No Kingdom of God for Softies? or, What Was Paul Really Saying? 1 Corinthians 6:9–10 in Context', *BTB* 34 (2004), 17–40

Ellis, J. Edward, *Paul and Ancient View of Sexual Desire: Paul's Sexual Ethics in 1 Thessalonians 4, 1 Corinthians 7 and Romans 1* (LNTS 354; London: T&T Clark, 2007)

Evans, Craig A., *Mark 8:27—16:20* (WBC 34B; Nashville: Nelson, 2001)

Fee, Gordon D., '1 Corinthians 7:1–7 Revisited', in *Paul and the Corinthians: Studies on a Community in Conflict: Essays in Honour of Margaret Thrall* (ed. Trevor J. Burke and J. Keith Elliott; NovTSup 109; Leiden: Brill, 2003), 197–213

Fee, Gordon D., *The First Epistle to the Corinthians* (NICNT; Grand Rapids: Eerdmans, 1987)

Fiore, Benjamin, *The Pastoral Epistles: First Timothy, Second Timothy, Titus* (SP 12; Collegeville: Liturgical Press, 2007)

Fitzmyer, Joseph A., 'The Matthean Divorce Texts and Some New Palestinian Evidence', in Joseph A. Fitzmyer, *To Advance the Gospel: New Testament Studies* (2nd edn; Grand Rapids: Eerdmans, 1998), 79–111

Foster, Paul, *Community, Law and Mission in Matthew's Gospel* (WUNT 2 177; Tübingen: Mohr Siebeck, 2004)

France, Richard T., *The Gospel of Mark* (NIGTC; Grand Rapids: Eerdmans, 2002)

France, Richard T., *The Gospel of Matthew* (NICNT; Grand Rapids: Eerdmans, 2007)

Franzmann, Majella, *Jesus in the Nag Hammadi Writings* (Edinburgh: T&T Clark, 1996)

Fredrickson, David E., 'A Friendly, Hellenic Response to Professor Sayler', *Dialog* 44 (2005), 93–4

Fredrickson, David E., 'Natural and Unnatural Use in Romans 1:24–27: Paul and the Philosophic Critique of Eros', in *Homosexuality, Science, and the 'Plain Sense' of Scripture* (ed. David L. Balch; Grand Rapids: Eerdmans, 2000), 197–222

Fredrickson, David E., 'Passionless Sex in 1 Thessalonians 4:4–5', *Word and World* 23 (2003), 23–30

Gagnon, Robert A. J., 'The Bible and Homosexual Practice' and 'Response to Dan O. Via', in Dan O. Via and Robert A. J. Gagnon, *Homosexuality and the Bible: Two Views* (Minneapolis: Fortress, 2003), 41–92, 99–105; and 'Notes to Gagnon's Essay in the Gagnon–Via *Two Views* Book', <http://www.robgagnon.net/2VOnlineNotes.htm>

Gagnon, Robert A. J., *The Bible and Homosexual Practice: Texts and Hermeneutics* (Nashville: Abingdon, 2001)

Gillihan, Yonder Moynihan, 'Jewish Laws on Illicit Marriage, the Defilement of Offspring, and the Holiness of the Temple: A New Halakic Interpretation of 1 Corinthians 7.14', *JBL* 121 (2002), 711–44

Gordon, J. Dorcas, *Sister or Wife? 1 Corinthians 7 and Cultural Anthropology* (JSNTSup 149; Sheffield: JSOT Press, 1997)

Gundry, Robert H., *Mark: A Commentary on His Apology for the Cross* (Grand Rapids: Eerdmans, 1993)

Gundry-Volf, Judith M., 'Controlling the Bodies: A Theological Profile of the Corinthian Sexual Ascetics (1 Cor 7)', in *The Corinthian Correspondence* (ed. R. Bieringer; BETL 125; Leuven: Peeters, 1996), 519–41

Gundry-Volf, Judith M., 'Male and Female in Creation and New Creation: Interpretations of Galatians 3.28c and 1 Corinthians 7', in *To Tell the Mystery: Essays on New Testament Eschatology in Honor of Robert H. Gundry* (ed. T. E. Schmidt and M. Silva; JSNTSup 100; Sheffield: JSOT Press, 1994), 95–121

Hagner, Donald A., *Matthew* (2 vols; WBC 33AB; Dallas: Word, 1993/1995)

Hanks, Thomas, 'Romans', in *The Queer Bible Commentary* (ed. D. Guest, R. E. Goss, M. West, T. Bohache; London: SCM Press, 2006), 582–605

Harrington, Daniel J., *Gospel of Matthew* (SP 1; Collegeville: Liturgical Press, 1991)

Harris, Murray J., *The Second Epistle to the Corinthians: A Commentary on the Greek Text* (Grand Rapids: Eerdmans, 2005)

Harvey, Anthony E., 'Genesis versus Deuteronomy? Jesus on Marriage and Divorce', in *The Gospels and the Scriptures of Israel* (ed. C. A. Evans and W. R. Stegner; JSNTSup 104/Studies in Scripture in Early Judaism and Christianity 3; Sheffield: JSOT Press, 1994), 55–65

Hays, Richard B., *The Moral Vision of the New Testament: A Contemporary Introduction to New Testament Ethics* (Edinburgh: T&T Clark, 1996)

Helminiak, Daniel, *What the Bible Really Says about Homosexuality* (Millennium Edition, updated and expanded; New Mexico: Alamo Square, 2000)

Hester, J. David, 'Eunuchs and the Postgender Jesus: Matthew 19.12 and Transgressive Sexualities', *JSNT* 28 (2005), 13–40

Horsley, Richard A., 'Spiritual Marriage with Sophia', *VC* 33 (1979), 32–7

Horst, Pieter W. van der, 'Celibacy in Early Judaism', *RB* 109 (2002), 390–402

Horst, Pieter W. van der, 'Sarah's Seminal Emission: Hebrews 11.11 in the Light of Ancient Embryology', in *Greeks, Romans and Christians: Essays in Honour of Abraham J. Malherbe* (ed. David L. Balch, Everett Ferguson and Wayne A. Meeks; Minneapolis: Fortress, 1990), 287–302

Hurd, John C., *The Origin of 1 Corinthians* (Macon: Mercer University Press, 1983; originally London: SPCK, 1965)

Instone-Brewer, David, 'Deuteronomy 24:1–4 and the Origin of the Jewish Divorce Certificate', *JJS* 49 (1998), 230–43

Instone-Brewer, David, *Divorce and Remarriage in the Bible: The Social and Literary Context* (Grand Rapids: Eerdmans, 2002)

Isaksson, Abel, *Marriage and Ministry in the New Temple: A Study with Special References to Mt. 19.13–22 and 1 Cor. 11.3–16* (ASNU 24; Lund: Gleerup; Copenhagen: Munksgaard, 1965)

Jewett, Robert, *Romans* (Hermeneia; Minneapolis: Fortress, 2007)

Jones, David C., 'A Note on the LXX of Malachi 2.16', *JBL* 109 (1990), 683–5

Käsemann, Ernst, 'The Problem of the Historical Jesus', in *Essays on New Testament Themes* (SBT 41; London: SCM Press, 1964), 15–47

Kodell, Jerome, 'The Celibacy Logion in Matthew 19:12', *BTB* 8.1 (1978), 19–23

Lefkowitz, Mary R. and Fant, Maureen B., *Women's Life in Greece and Rome: A Source Book in Translation* (Baltimore: Johns Hopkins University Press, 1982)

Levine, Amy-Jill, 'The Word Becomes Flesh: Jesus, Gender, and Sexuality', in *Jesus Two Thousand Years Later* (ed. James H. Charlesworth; Harrisburg: Trinity Press International, 2000), 62–83

Loader, William, 'Challenged at the Boundaries: A Conservative Jesus in Mark's Tradition', *JSNT* 63 (1996), 45–61

Loader, William, *The Dead Sea Scrolls on Sexuality: Attitudes towards Sexuality in Sectarian and Related Literature at Qumran* (Grand Rapids: Eerdmans, 2009)

Loader, William, *Enoch, Levi, and Jubilees on Sexuality: Attitudes towards Sexuality in the Early Enoch Literature, the Aramaic Levi Document, and the Book of Jubilees* (Grand Rapids: Eerdmans, 2007)

Loader, William, *Jesus and the Fundamentalism of His Day* (Grand Rapids: Eerdmans, 2001)

Loader, William, *Jesus' Attitude towards the Law: A Study of the Gospels* (WUNT 2.97; Tübingen: Mohr Siebeck, 1997; Grand Rapids: Eerdmans, 2002)

Loader, William, *Philo, Josephus and the Testaments on Sexuality* (Grand Rapids: Eerdmans, forthcoming)

Loader, William, *The Pseudepigrapha on Sexuality: Attitudes towards Sexuality in Apocalypses, Testaments, Legends, Wisdom, and Related Literature* (Grand Rapids: Eerdmans, forthcoming)

Loader, William, *Septuagint, Sexuality, and the New Testament* (Grand Rapids: Eerdmans, 2004)

Loader, William, *Sexuality and the Jesus Tradition* (Grand Rapids: Eerdmans, 2005)

Luz, Ulrich, *Matthew* (3 vols; Hermeneia; Minneapolis: Fortress, 1989, 2001, 2005)

MacDonald, Dennis R., *There is No Male and Female: The Fate of a Dominical Saying in Paul and Gnosticism* (Philadelphia: Fortress, 1987)

MacDonald, Margaret Y., *Colossians and Ephesians* (SP 17; Collegeville: Liturgical Press, 2000)

Marshall, Mary J., 'Jesus and the Banquets: An Investigation of the Early Christian Tradition concerning Jesus' Presence at Banquets with Toll Collectors and Sinners' (Diss. Murdoch University, 2002)

Martin, Dale B., '*Arsenokoitês* and *Malakos*: Meaning and Consequences', in Dale B. Martin, *Sex and the Single Savior: Gender and Sexuality in Biblical Interpretation* (Louisville: Westminster John Knox, 2006), 37–50

Martin, Dale B., *The Corinthian Body* (New Haven: Yale University Press, 1995)

Martin, Dale B., 'Heterosexism and its Interpretation of Romans 1:18–32', in Dale B. Martin, *Sex and the Single Savior: Gender and Sexuality in Biblical Interpretation* (Louisville: Westminster John Knox, 2006), 51–64

Martin, Dale B., 'Paul Without Passion: on Paul's Rejection of Desire in Sex and Marriage', in Dale B. Martin, *Sex and the Single Savior: Gender and Sexuality in Biblical Interpretation* (Louisville: Westminster John Knox, 2006), 65–76

Mason, Stephen, 'What Josephus Says About the Essenes in his Judean War', in *Text and Artifact in the Religions of Mediterranean Antiquity: Essays in Honour of Peter Richardson* (ed. S. Wilson and M. Desjardins; Waterloo, Ont.: Wilfrid Laurier University Press, 2000), 423–55

Matera, Frank J., *II Corinthians: A Commentary* (Louisville: Westminster John Knox, 2003)

Meeks, Wayne A., 'The Image of the *Androgyne*: Some Uses of a Symbol in Earliest Christianity', *HR* 13 (1974), 165–208

Meier, John P., *A Marginal Jew: Rethinking the Historical Jesus*, vol. 3: *Companions and Competitors* (ABRL; New York: Doubleday, 2001)

Meier, John P., *A Marginal Jew: Rethinking the Historical Jesus*, vol. 4: *Law and Love* (AYBRL; New Haven: Yale University Press, 2009)

Metzger, Bruce, *A Textual Commentary on the Greek New Testament* (2nd edn; London/New York: United Bible Societies, 1994)

Miller, James E., 'Response: Pederasty and Romans 1:27: A Response to Mark Smith', *JAAR* 65 (1997), 861–6

Moloney, Francis J., 'Matthew 19:3–12 and Celibacy', in Francis J. Moloney, '*A Hard Saying*': *The Gospel and Culture* (Collegeville: Liturgical Press, 2001), 35–52

Neirynck, Frans, 'The Sayings of Jesus in 1 Corinthians', in *The Corinthian Correspondence* (ed. R. Bieringer; BETL 125; Leuven: Peeters, 1996), 141–76

Newton, Michael, *The Concept of Purity at Qumran and in the Letters of Paul* (SNTSMS 53; Cambridge: Cambridge University Press, 1985)

Nissinen, Martti, *Homoeroticism in the Biblical World: A Historical Perspective* (Minneapolis: Fortress, 1998)

Nolland, John, *The Gospel of Matthew: A Commentary on the Greek Text* (NIGTC; Grand Rapids: Eerdmans; Bletchley: Paternoster, 2005)

Nolland, John, 'The Gospel Prohibition of Divorce: Tradition History and Meaning', *JSNT* 58 (1995), 19–35

Nolland, John, 'Romans 1:26–27 and the Homosexuality Debate', *HBT* 22 (2000), 32–57

Økland, Jorunn, *Women in Their Place: Paul and the Corinthians Discourse of Gender and Sanctuary Space* (JSNTSup 269; London: T&T Clark, 2004)

Olson, Daniel C., '"Those who have not defiled themselves with women": Revelation 14:4 and the Book of Enoch', *CBQ* 59 (1997), 492–510

Osiek, Carolyn and Balch, David L., *Families in the New Testament World: Households and House Churches* (Louisville: Westminster John Knox, 1997)

Osiek, Carolyn and MacDonald, Margaret Y., *A Woman's Place: House Churches in Earliest Christianity* (Minneapolis: Fortress, 2006)

Oster, Richard E., 'Use, Misuse and Neglect of Archaeological Evidence in Some Modern Works on 1 Corinthians (1 Cor 7,1–5; 8,10; 11,2–16; 12,14–26)', *ZNW* 83 (1992), 52–73

Phipps, William E., *The Sexuality of Jesus: Theological and Literary Perspectives* (New York: Harper & Row, 1993)

Poirier, John C. and Frankovic, Joseph, 'Celibacy and Charism in 1 Cor 7:5–7', *HTR* 89 (1996), 1–18

Quesnell, Quenton, '"Made themselves Eunuchs for the Kingdom of Heaven" (Mt 19.12)', *CBQ* 30 (1968), 335–58

Richard, Earl, *First and Second Thessalonians* (SP 11; Collegeville: Liturgical Press, 1995)

Rosner, Brian S., *Paul, Scripture and Ethics: A Study of 1 Corinthians 5–7* (AGJU 22; Leiden: Brill, 1994)

Rosner, Brian S., 'Temple Prostitution in 1 Corinthians 6.12–20', *NovT* 40 (1998), 336–51

Saldarini, Anthony J., *Matthew's Christian–Jewish Community* (Chicago: University of Chicago Press, 1994)

Sanders, E. P., *Jesus and Judaism* (London: SCM Press, 1985)

Satlow, Michael L., *Jewish Marriage in Antiquity* (Princeton: Princeton University Press, 2001)

Sayler, Gwendolyn B., 'Beyond the Biblical Impasse: Homosexuality through the Lens of Theological Anthropology', *Dialog* 44 (2005), 81–9

Schoedel, William R., 'Same-Sex Eros: Paul and the Greco-Roman Tradition', in *Homosexuality, Science, and the 'Plain Sense' of Scripture* (ed. David L. Balch; Grand Rapids: Eerdmans, 2000), 43–72

Schüssler Fiorenza, Elisabeth, *In Memory of Her: A Feminist Theological Reconstruction of Christian Origins* (New York: Crossroad, 1985)

Scroggs, Robin, *The New Testament and Homosexuality: Contextual Background for Contemporary Debate* (Philadelphia: Fortress, 1983)

Senior, Donald P., *1 Peter* and Daniel J. Harrington, *Jude and 2 Peter* (SP 15; Collegeville: Liturgical Press, 2003)

Sigal, Phillip, *The Halakhah of Jesus of Nazareth according to the Gospel of Matthew* (SBL 18; Atlanta: SBL, 2007)

Skinner, Marilyn B., *Sexuality in Greek and Roman Culture* (Oxford: Blackwell, 2005)

Smith, Mark D., 'Ancient Bisexuality and the Interpretation of Romans 1:26–27', *JAAR* 64 (1996), 223–56

Smith, Morton, *The Secret Gospel: The Discovery and Interpretation of the Secret Gospel according to Mark* (New York: Harper & Row, 1973)

Snodgrass, Klyne R., 'Matthew and the Law', in *Treasures Old and New: Contributions to Matthean Studies* (ed. D. R. Bauer and M. A. Powell; SBLSymS 1; Atlanta: Scholars Press, 1996), 111–18

Streete, Gail C., *The Strange Woman: Power and Sex in the Bible* (Louisville: Westminster John Knox, 1999)

Swancutt, Diana M., '"The Disease of Effemination": The Charge of Effeminacy and the Verdict of God (Romans 1:18—2:16)', in *New Testament Masculinities* (ed. Stephen D. Moore and Janice Capel Anderson; SBLSemS 45; Atlanta: SBL, 2003), 193–234

Thiselton, Anthony C., *The First Epistle to the Corinthians: A Commentary on the Greek Text* (NIGTC; Grand Rapids: Eerdmans; Carlisle: Paternoster, 2000)

Toit, Andrie B. du, 'Paul, Homosexuality and Christian Ethics', in *Neotestamentica et Philonica: Studies in Honour of Peder Borgen* (ed. David E. Aune; Leiden: Brill, 2003), 92–107

Vermes, Geza, *Jesus the Jew: A Historian's Reading of the Gospels* (London: Collins, 1973)

Via, Dan O., 'The Bible, the Church, and Homosexuality' and 'Response to Robert A. J. Gagnon', in Dan O. Via and Robert A. J. Gagnon, *Homosexuality and the Bible: Two Views* (Minneapolis: Fortress, 2003), 1–39, 93–8

Via, Dan O., *The Ethics of Mark's Gospel in the Middle of Time* (Philadelphia: Fortress, 1985)

Wanamaker, Charles A., *The Epistles to the Thessalonians* (NIGTC; Grand Rapids: Eerdmans, 1990)

Ward, Roy Bowen, 'Why Unnatural? The Tradition behind Romans 1:26–27', *HTR* 90 (1997), 263–84

Watson, Alan, 'Jesus and the Adulteress', *Bib* 80 (1999), 100–8

Watson, Francis, *Agape, Eros, Gender: Towards a Pauline Sexual Ethic* (Cambridge: Cambridge University Press, 2000)

Watson, Francis, 'The Authority of the Voice: A Theological Reading of 1 Cor 11.2–16', *NTS* 46 (2000), 520–36

Williams, Craig A., *Roman Homosexuality: Ideologies of Masculinity in Classical Antiquity* (Oxford: Oxford University Press, 1999)

Bibliography

Wimbush, Vincent L., *Paul, the Worldly Ascetic: Response to the World and Self-Understanding according to 1 Corinthians 7* (Macon: Mercer University Press, 1987), 50–62

Wink, Walter, *Engaging the Powers* (Minneapolis: Fortress, 1992)

Winter, Bruce, '1 Corinthians 7:6–7: A Caveat and a Framework for "The Sayings" in 7:8–24', *TynBul* 48 (1997), 57–65

Winter, Bruce W., *Roman Wives, Roman Widows: The Appearance of New Women and the Pauline Communities* (Grand Rapids: Eerdmans, 2003)

Winter, Bruce, 'Secular and Christian Responses to Corinthian Famines', *TynBul* 40 (1989), 86–106

Wire, Antoinette C., *The Corinthian Women Prophets: A Reconstruction through Paul's Rhetoric* (Minneapolis: Augsburg Fortress, 1990)

Witherington, Ben, 'Matthew 5.32 and 19.9 – Exception or Exceptional Situation', *NTS* 31 (1985), 571–6

Witherington, Ben, *Women in the Earliest Churches* (SNTSMS 59; Cambridge: Cambridge University Press, 1988)

Witherington, Ben, *Women in the Ministry of Jesus* (SNTSMS 51; Cambridge: Cambridge University Press, 1984)

Wright, David F., 'Homosexuals or Prostitutes? The Meaning of ARSENOKOITAI (1 Cor 6:9; 1 Tim 1:10)', *VC* 38 (1984), 124–53

Yarbrough, O. Larry, *Not Like the Gentiles: Marriage Rules in the Letters of Paul* (SBLDS 80; Atlanta: Scholars Press, 1985)

Index of ancient and biblical sources

Index of ancient and biblical sources

*Theophilus of
  Antioch*   131 n. 106

OTHER WRITINGS

Epictetus

Discourses
*3.22.67–76; 3.24.60;
  4.7.5*   112

Josephus

Against Apion
2.25   139 n. 7
2.199   10

Antiquities
4.254–6   40
6.69–72   68

Jewish War
1.277   40
2.119–61   102
2.160–1   102, 119

Philo

On Abraham
134–7   10

Contemplative Life
*1–2; 11–40;
  63–90*   102
63   9

Decalogue
121   71

*Every Good Man is
Free*
75–91   102

On Joseph
44   139 n. 7

Life of Moses
2.68–9   114, 117

*Posterity and Exile
of Cain*
78   114

Special Laws
3.30–1   82
3.37–42   9
3.112   100

Plato

Laws
836C   9,
  130 n. 68
838   18

Symposium   9

Pliny

Natural History
5.17.4   102

Plutarch

Moralia
140D   52

**RABBINIC
LITERATURE**

Mishnah

Abot
1.5   90

Gittin
9.10   82

Niddah
2.1   138

Sanhedrin
6.4; 7.2; 7.3
  139 n. 7

Yebamot
8.4   107

Zabim
2.1   107

Babylonian Talmud

Abodah Zarah
8a   139 n. 7

Gittin
90a   82

Ketubbot
62b   138

Niddah
13a–b   138

Shabbath
17a   31

Sanhedrin
15a   139 n. 7
41ab   139 n. 7
82a   31

Sukkah
29a   31

Yebamot
75a 79b   107

Index of modern authors

Allison, D. C. 40, 82, 90, 133, 137, 138, 139, 140, 141, 142, 143, 144
Aune, D. E. 144

Balch, D. L. 48, 101, 116, 133, 134, 135, 143, 145, 146, 147
Banks, R. 136, 142
Barton, S. C. 141
Baumert, N. 145
Beattie, G. 48, 56, 133, 134, 135, 136
Betz, H. D. 137, 138, 139, 141, 142
Blinzler, J. 144
Blomberg, C. L. 141, 142, 143, 144
Bockmuehl, M. 142
Boswell, J. 20, 21, 25, 30, 31, 129, 130, 131
Brooten, B. J. 18, 20, 21, 24, 28, 128, 129, 130, 131
Byrne, B. 128

Caragounis, C. C. 144, 145, 146
Carter, W. 137
Cartlidge, D. R. 147
Catchpole, D. R. 139, 141, 143
Collins, R. F. 42, 52, 56, 58, 94, 129, 131, 132, 135, 136, 138, 139, 142, 143, 145, 146, 147
Countryman, L. W. 13, 44, 127, 128, 132, 134, 137, 141, 142, 143, 145
Crossan, J. D. 147

Darko, D. K. 135, 136
Davies, W. D. 40, 82, 90, 133, 137, 138, 139, 140, 141, 142, 143, 144
Deming, W. 42, 46, 70, 77, 110, 111, 113, 133, 134, 138, 140, 145, 146, 147
Derrett, J. D. M. 138
Dixon, S. 134, 141
Donahue, J. R. and Harrington, D. J. 138

Dover, K. J. 22, 129
Dunn, J. D. G. 128

Ellens, J. H. 98, 143
Elliott, J. H. 31, 129, 131, 132
Ellis, J. E. 46, 77, 130, 134
Evans, C. A. 138

Fee, G. D. 135, 142, 143, 144, 145
Fiore, B. 55, 135
Fitzmyer, J. A. 96, 141, 142, 143, 144
Foster, P. 137
France, R. T. 136, 138, 141, 142, 144
Franzmann, M. 147
Fredrickson, D. E. 26, 46, 77, 130, 131, 134, 139

Gagnon, R. A. J. 7, 15, 21, 23, 24, 26, 27, 28, 45, 127, 128, 129, 130, 131, 132, 134
Gillihan, Y. M. 43, 133
Gordon, J. D. 143, 146, 147
Gundry, R. H. 133, 138, 140, 141, 143
Gundry-Volf, J. M. 47, 134, 136, 143, 145, 146, 147

Hagner, D. A. 137, 141
Hanks, T. 127, 128, 129, 132
Harrington, D. J. 135
Harris, M. J. 138
Harvey, A. E. 84, 90, 140, 141
Hays, R. B. 28, 130, 131, 132, 140, 141, 143, 145
Helminiak, D. 24, 128, 130, 132
Hester, J. D. 107, 132, 144
Horsley, R. A. 146
Horst, P. W. van der 134, 144, 147
Hurd, J. C. 146, 147

Index of subjects

Adam, fall of 21, 28
adultery 4, 10, 21–2, 32, 34, 40, 57,
    61–8, 70–1, 77; and divorce 62,
    81–3, 87–97; and uncleanness 62
anal sex 18, 19–20, 25
angels *see* watchers
anger of God 14–15
Antipas 34, 72, 95
Aristotle 48
arsenokoitai 30–3
attitude 63–5, 122

Babatha archive 40, 83
beloved disciple 33
Ben Sira 38
bestiality 124
betrothal 36–7
Bible 2–3
bride price 37

celibacy 11, 19, 34, 41, 46–9, 56, 65,
    74, 91, 93–4, 98, 101, 102, 104–19,
    121, 124–6
centurion's servant 33
childbirth 42–4, 56, 124
commandments 61–2
conception 18, 25, 43, 56, 79, 119
contraception 4, 18
cosmetics and jewellery 52
creation 14, 24, 27–8, 44–7, 121
Cynics 46, 110, 113–14

Damascus Document 11, 16
daughters 4, 37–8
desire 16–17, 19, 25–6, 29, 46–7, 66,
    77, 111
dogs 34
divorce 4, 80–97, 111, 121–2, 124;
    exception 88–91; indissolubility
    83–8; *see also* adultery: and
    divorce

divorcees 40–1, 61
dowry 37

Epicurus 109
Essenes 102, 118
eunuch 33, 45, 106–7
excess 26–7, 29, 46, 77
excision 68–71
eyes 66–7

feminization, effeminate 8, 16, 20,
    21, 24–5, 30–2
fertility 43

gender roles 24–7, 35
genitalia 1, 24, 27, 70
Gentiles 12–13, 24–5
Gnosticism 36

hermeneutics 1–6, 7–8, 123–6
homosexual *see* same-sex relations
honour/shame 16–17, 19, 20, 25,
    29
household 3, 4, 37–8, 121
household codes: Colossians 48–9;
    Ephesians 49–51; 1 Peter,
    Titus 51–2
husband 48–53
hypocrisy 12–13

idolatry 12, 14–15, 20
incest 34, 71, 74, 75, 90, 91, 95, 107
inheritance 4
intermarriage 74–5
interpretation *see* hermeneutics

Jesus 34, 44–5, 60, 107, 116–17; on
    law 64–5
John the Baptist 34, 64, 74, 92, 95,
    117, 125
Joseph and Aseneth 35